THE ART OF THE BUSINESS LUNCH

Building Relationships
Between 12 and 2

Robin Jay

CAREER
PRESS
Franklin Lakes, NJ

THE ART OF THE BUSINESS LUNCH
EDITED BY CHRISTOPHER CAROLEI
TYPESET BY EILEEN DOW MUNSON
Cover design by Mada Design, Inc./NYC
Printed in the U.S.A. by Book-mart Press

To order this title, please call toll-free 1-800-CAREER-1 (NJ and Canada: 201-848-0310) to order using VISA or MasterCard, or for further information on books from Career Press.

CAREER
PRESS

The Career Press, Inc., 3 Tice Road, PO Box 687,
Franklin Lakes, NJ 07417
www.careerpress.com

Library of Congress Cataloging-in-Publication Data

Jay, Robin.
    The art of the business lunch : building relationships between 12 and 2 / Robin Jay.
        p.cm.
    Includes index.
    ISBN 1-56414-851-3 (paper)
        1. Business etiquette. 2. Business entertaining. 3. Employment interviewing. I. Title.

    HF5389.J39 2006
    395.5'20--dc22   2005050776

*This book is dedicated
to the memory of Murphy,
who loved a great lunch as much as I do.*

Acknowledgments

Thank you to my family—although different from each other in every way, they all agree on the facts that I love to sell, and I know a great lunch. In particular, thanks to my sister, Terri, who has always been a great source of encouragement; to my brother, Barry (the flyer), who quotes *Star Wars* logic to help me; to my brother, James, who also sells for a living, and is always a light in my life; and to my parents, Erwin and Love. Thank you to each of you for being there for me.

A thank you also goes out to my friends who helped me with this book—Sharon, Michele, Teri, Robyn, Matisun, and Gordon—and all of my friends who ever said a positive word or expressed belief in me. I don't know how anyone could succeed without the help of friends like you and the support you have given me along the way. And a special thanks to my wonderful artist, Bill Verrill, who is a genius at turning concept into form.

I'd also like to thank everyone with whom I've ever had the pleasure of dining. If you think you see yourself in a story, you are probably right.

And one last word of appreciation (though they will never know about it), to Gracie and Georgie, who inspired me to spend more time at home—writing.

Contents

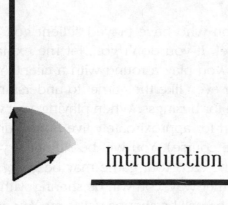

Introduction

I worked as an advertising account executive for more than 18 years. During that time I took clients out to lunch more than 3,000 times. That's a lot of lunch!

Through the years I have learned what works, and what doesn't. I have built and sustained successful professional and personal relationships that have helped me to grow my sales by more than 2000 percent! In addition, I have earned the reputation of "the Queen of the Business Lunch" in my hometown of Las Vegas. My friends and associates call me constantly for advice on where to go, and what to do.

In *The Art of the Business Lunch*, I will teach you specific ways to cater to your clients that will help you to build more substantial and profitable relationships. One of the best ways to bond with your clients is by taking them to lunch. When you introduce a social situation into a business relationship, you change the dynamic you have with your client by building a stronger foundation. I originally made this discovery by playing client golf.

Those of you who have played "client golf" already know the secret. If you don't golf, let me explain what happens when you play a round with a client. You don't have to play, or even like the game, to understand why it is a great game for business. When playing, you will likely share a golf cart for approximately five hours (unless you opt to walk the course). You will be sitting very close to each other in the cart. Your game may be going great, or not so well—either way, you will be sharing with your client, and he or she will be sharing with you. You can *not* sit that close to someone for that long without learning a few things about him or her, and vice versa.

If your client is unhappy at his or her job, unhappy at home, or encountering a rough patch, odds are you will learn something about it. I have found out things about my clients that I might never have come to know otherwise—usually more business-related, rather than personal, but a fair mix of both. I have learned that they may be looking for a new job, or that their boss is looking for a new job. Any detail of someone's personal or professional life may come out during a round of golf.

The biggest challenges are to practice discretion, to focus on your game, and to be a great host or hostess. By accomplishing these three things, you will be able to cut through the corporate clouds and discover the real people you are working with. In doing so, you can learn insights about your clients that will help you to better work with them.

But not everyone plays golf. So how do get your clients who don't play golf to reveal a part of their inner self, and let down some walls? Take them to lunch!

The miracle of lunch

Food is the ultimate common denominator among people. We all have to eat. Whether we choose to eat healthy, poorly, or somewhere inbetween, we all eat. And sharing a meal with someone will forever change your relationship with that person. You may end up liking him more, or you may end up liking him less. You may gain or lose respect for someone based on the information she shares, or how she behaves in a restaurant. Good or bad—you will learn a lot about that person! If you know how to treat the person, and how to draw out his or her personality, you will find that you may start to *prefer* to share a meal with someone before doing business with him or her. Sharing a meal with someone is the fastest way to find out what kind of person he or she is—it strips away all veneers and reveals what's underneath.

This is the primary reason that some executives prefer to interview job applicants during a lunch meeting. Doing so can be very revealing. Who would have thought that magic could happen over a sandwich?

If you don't believe the difference that sharing a meal with someone can have on a relationship, just perform a Google search for "breaking bread," and read some of the more than *one million* responses! From biblical references, to turning a house into a home, breaking bread with someone is indeed a miraculous experience, and one that will forever transform your relationship.

In this book, you will learn the right way to conduct business lunches so as to net quantifiable results for you in your billing, client satisfaction, and overall success.

Would you like to improve your business relationships and generate more sales? How about your job satisfaction? Are you enjoying your work and your business?

Once you learn the importance and effectiveness of breaking bread with your clients, you will see signs of improvement in your sales, in your business, and—surprisingly—in your personal life, too. Learning how to personalize your business by taking your clients to lunch will bring you greater satisfaction on all fronts. However, there is a right way and a wrong way to conduct business at the table.

A lot can go wrong, and I will tell you what to watch out for. What entrée should you never order at a business lunch? Is it ever okay to have a cocktail at noon? Is it okay to discuss your love life, or to tell a dirty joke? How do you know if your behavior will be acceptable? Does what you wear to a business lunch really make a difference?

We've all known associates and peers who don't seem to have much more going for them than anyone else. And yet these people are loved by their clients, write more business, and find more success and happiness than the rest of the pack. The reason is often because these people have found a way to make their clients feel special, and so their clients prefer to work with them rather than the competition.

Change your perspective and put yourself in your client's shoes. See things from his or her point of view. When you do so, you will find the way to make your clients like and respect you, and feel good about doing so. If you cater to your client's needs first, your needs will ultimately be met as well—you will find more clients, and, subsequently, more success.

Having genuine concern about others will also fill you with passion for your work. Instead of just conducting business, you will become involved in people's lives. Your reputation as someone who cares about the people in your life, and who has their best interests at heart, will grow. Make your clients feel special, and they will go out of their way to work with you.

Sharing a meal with others is one of the fastest ways to get to know them. Nothing is quite as revealing as one's conduct at the table. Art Fettig, of Growth Unlimited, said that several years ago he had a business lunch with the president of a corporation that produced subliminal audio tapes. Fettig had considered collaborating with the company to produce audio tapes for children. However, he felt hesitant about the deal when something happened that finally convinced him to say no.

The waitress had wheeled out a dessert cart that displayed about a dozen items. The president told the waitress to pack up one of each of the over-priced items to go. He was taking home a treat and was charging it to his expense account.

Art thought that the firm would not be around very long (if the president's behavior was any indication of its business practices), and six months later it indeed filed for bankruptcy. Art could have had many meetings with that man in his company's offices and never have been able to discover the fabric of his ethics as quickly as Art had at just one luncheon!

Just as a game of golf can, a business lunch can be very revealing. In a relaxed atmosphere, most people will let their guard down a little. This is usually a very good thing for bonding and building relationships, as well as for seeing what someone is really all about.

I recently read a passage from bestselling author John Kremer. He stated in one of his newsletters, "All of marketing, all of business, can be broken down to one thing: creating relationships—or, as I like to put it, making friends. Your job is to make friends."

When I first read that statement, I was caught off guard. He had come right out and said something I had believed for so long, and with no apologies for it. I think it's easier for us to refer to our primary business goal, whether in sales, management, or any other relationship-based business, as "creating relationships." But the more I thought about it, the more I am sure that Kremer is right.

As I mentioned, people like to do business with people they like. It stands to reason that people do, indeed, like their friends. So to become friends with, or at least become "friendly" with, your clients is the key to successful business. Jeffrey Gitomer, author of *The Little Red Book of Selling,* puts it this way: "If you make a sale, you can earn a commission. If you make a friend, you can earn a fortune."

Confiding secrets, or sharing ideas, expectations, disappointments, and other personal experiences is easy to do over salads and steaks. It's important to learn what information you can volunteer and what you should keep to yourself. Even though you are building a relationship, and hope that it will eventually become a friendship, you still need to be discreet. Just as you wouldn't discuss your "dirty laundry" with a stranger, you shouldn't ever discuss problems at work—especially with a new client. If your client, however, wants to share his or her trials and tribulations with you, that's another thing altogether.

Most people enjoy a good visit, and you can find out all sorts of things that you might never come to know without such an intimate setting. However, remember that the rules of conduct are different for a business lunch, and what applies to you does *not* apply to your clients!

In *The Art of the Business Lunch* I will also help you to achieve a better "feel" for your clients, but I will also teach you *specific* ways to achieve better results with your business relationships.

Every year that I have worked in sales I have grown my accounts. I have become friends with my clients, as well as with their bosses and associates. Have you ever had someone introduce you to their boss or coworker with such enthusiasm that you immediately like and accept the new man or woman? You "grandfather them" in to your circle because they came so highly recommended! And later, as you get to know them, you begin to understand why they are so popular and friendly. Whenever you are with them, you feel great about yourself and your friendship with this person.

For some people, the ability to make others feel good about themselves comes naturally. But many more have an extremely hard time in some social or professional situations. Now you can learn not just how to fit in, but how to focus on others—which in turn makes others feel better about you.

I will even guide you through that scary, haunted forest we call the "battle of the sexes." Think this doesn't exist anymore? You're wrong! In *EVEolution: The Eight*

Truths of Marketing to Women (Hyperion, 2000), by Faith Popcorn and Lys Marigold, the authors make the following observation: "Men and women don't think the same way, don't communicate the same way, don't buy for the same reasons... He simply wants the transaction to take place. She's interested in creating a relationship. *Every place women go, they make connections.*"

On the other hand, men can play a "pickup" game of basketball at the gym, and suddenly become buddies during a court game. So, who has the upper hand when it comes to building relationships?

We've all heard the claim of John Gray, Ph.d., that "men are from Mars" and "women are from Venus." And I don't know anyone who disagrees that men and women are different! It stands to reason that these differences between the sexes must also be taken into consideration in our business relationships. And, because lunch, breakfast, and dinner are social situations, the lines must be drawn from the beginning, and respected. In Chapter 7, I will teach you some of the differences in how men and women communicate, and what they could mean to you during a client lunch.

I will also teach you some simple ways to avoid awkward first meetings. If you've ever wondered whether you should pick up your client at his or her office, or meet him or her at the restaurant, I will explain how to make your choice. Do you think the restaurant you choose makes a difference? You bet! What about cell phone etiquette? Who can talk on their phone as long as they like? The details you've wondered about can mean the difference between just having a bite to eat with a client and building a solid foundation for a long-lasting relationship.

Once you understand *how* important it is to become good at building relationships, it will make learning how to build them at lunch even easier. I have learned the art of the business lunch, and can teach you how to increase your sales, cement your relationships, and make lunch the most productive and enjoyable time of your business day. Oh, and being from Las Vegas, I'm willing to bet on it!

Chapter 1

Why All the Fuss?

*People would rather
do business with
people they like.*

How did the business lunch become such a big deal? The politically incorrect three-martini lunch is a thing of the past, as is "power lunching." Business lunches have evolved into a regular, acceptable part of business in the last 40 years. Money and careers can be made or lost because of relationships, and the ability to build strong relationships has become an important part of business. People prefer to do business with people they like. You can make yourself invaluable to your clients by making them feel special when you take them to lunch and treat them right. They will prefer to do business with *you!*

The fast pace of business leaves many executives tired and emotionally drained. When you learn how to bring excitement, energy, and fun into someone's day, he or she will soon begin to look forward to visiting with you. Let's face it: Our clients have a lot of choices—regardless of what product or service they need. For some, the choice of which company they choose to work with may simply come down to price. If budget is a client's only concern, then, as a sales rep, your best hope of getting his or her business may be found in offering the lowest price (or even offering adding value).

However, in *many* situations, a decision-maker will have enough flexibility that he or she can choose to work with a preferred salesperson. Scott McKain, author of *All Business Is Show Business* (Rutledge Hill Press, 2002), suggests approaching business in a different way: "The purpose of any business is to profitably create emotional connections that are so compelling to customers and employees that loyalty is assured."

Knowing how to create "quality time," and an emotional connection with your clients, will enable you to take your business relationships to a higher level—and that will result in increased sales. And, as an added bonus, you will likely find that you will *enjoy* your work more, too.

By knowing what to say, and how to help your clients relax—especially at lunchtime—you can set the mood for some serious bonding. Nothing creates solid relationships the way spending quality time together can, and a business lunch can be that quality time. Once you learn to personalize your business, a prospect or client will be more likely to accept a phone call from you, especially if the two of you recently enjoyed a great lunch together.

Knowing how effective a lunchtime strategy can be, and the impact that it can have on your business, why then would so many executives still prefer to eat lunch at their desk, do paperwork, meet their friends for lunch, or grab a bite at the drive-thru? The answer is simple: For most people, taking a stranger to lunch is as much fun as a blind date! It can be awkward, uncomfortable, weird, or just plain unsettling.

Lauren, a California business owner, shared her reaction with me when she heard me talking about business lunches, and job interview lunches in particular. Even though she had been running a home-based business for more than a decade, and was long out of the traditional job market, she confessed, "I immediately re-experienced the panic I used to feel whenever I had something at stake and eating was involved." She went on to say, "I have always been too anxious to eat in these circumstances, fearing the insides of the sandwich would dribble out, or food would stick between my teeth, or I would eat too slowly and be the last one at the table—all of which has happened to me. I was interviewed that way once and ordered something very bland and light, but it only added to my tension."

Lauren also recounted some past job experiences where lunch had played a crucial, and uncomfortable role.

"At one job," she said. "I coordinated lunch meetings for a group of doctors. I was supposed to eat with them as well. I never ordered a sandwich for myself, and I always got annoying comments, too. In the one situation I was asked, 'Is that all you're going to eat?' Another time said, 'You're not eating, Lauren? Why not?'"

Lauren is not alone. But at least she was aware that there was a problem, and she has worked hard to overcome it. Many people don't understand how important it is to be prepared and participate at a lunch.

You can overcome the awkwardness or discomfort that you usually feel when you are out to lunch with strangers, because you *know* that taking clients to lunch will help you to build your business, increase your sales, and even make you feel better. So why are you still reluctant to do so? Does your reluctance go beyond being uncomfortable or awkward? Could it be out-and-out fear?

Napoleon Hill's classic book, *Think and Grow Rich* (Ballantine Books, 1987), originally published way back in 1937, identified six ghosts of fear to which any of us can fall prey. Every fear that we have can be traced back to one of these "ghosts." The list includes three that are health-related: fear of ill health; fear of old age; and fear of death. The other three are the fear of losing someone's love, the fear of poverty, and the fear of criticism. (Note: After having left the United States for the first time, he added a seventh fear: fear of the loss of liberty.) If you've never read this book, you should treat yourself to a copy. It is brilliant.

The reason I mention this book is because knowing more about your fears helps you to control them. If you are like Lauren, and the thought of having to take a client or prospect out to lunch terrifies you, ask yourself why. When you look at Hill's list of the seven ghosts of fear, which category does "fear of taking a client to lunch" fall into? Obviously, the answer is "fear of criticism."

I think we have all suffered "fear of criticism" at some time. There are so many things that can go wrong at a business meeting that is held in an office—but conducting business during a meal presents its own challenges. As Lauren said, "What if the insides of my sandwich fall out as I take a bite?" That's just the beginning! What if you knock over your drink, spill on yourself, or have food in your teeth as you review your presentation? There are indeed hundreds of things that can (and *do*) go wrong *all the time!* We are human beings who make mistakes, spill drinks, and get food stuck in our teeth. If you let your fear get to you, you are going to miss out on what could be the most rewarding part of your career—sharing with other human beings. So, try to remember that we *all* suffer from each of these fears (to some degree), and that we are all capable of overcoming them.

I'm sure it helps to know you are not alone—we all have fears.

In Hawaii a few years ago, I was teamed up for a golf outing with a husband and wife, and their talented, 12-year old son. It can be hard to play with strangers, especially when you're not at the top of your game. And golf is a sport where the harder you try, the worse you are likely to play. I was nervous and afraid I wouldn't hit the ball well, especially because I was playing with three strangers. Sure enough, my first shot was dreadful.

I nearly died of embarrassment when my ball skidded down the fairway, going only about 40 yards—I wanted to run and hide. I couldn't believe I had attempted to play with strangers, and I was sure they would not be as kind as my friends back home. The husband watched my shot and said jokingly, "I've never done that before." His sarcasm instantly melted my fears. Of *course* he had! *Anyone* who has ever played golf, even the professionals, has hit a lousy shot on occasion—especially from the first tee. I knew then that I was with friends, and that my fears had been unfounded. (And, fortunately, my game picked up when I was finally able to relax.) We all had a good laugh at my shot. I took a Mulligan (or free shot) to make up for that lousy first drive and proceeded down the fairway.

I can remember standing on the first tee box, wishing I was a better golfer. I was hoping for a "crushing drive," so my partners wouldn't dread having to play with me. I was totally consumed with my own fear of criticism. I know what it feels like to experience the fear that undermines confidence. I believe that is the same fear that keeps professionals at their desks during lunch. (Or at the drive-thru, reading a book during lunchtime, or dining exclusively with their friends.) Had I known deep inside that I was a consistently great golfer, I would not have been afraid as I took my shot.

Knowing what you are doing is the best way to gain the confidence to handle any situation effectively, and I can help you to become knowledgeable about how to handle a business lunch.

So, what makes a great lunch? It's the perfect combination of business, entertainment, compassion, encouragement, or whatever else your client is in the mood for. Finding common ground is very important in any relationship (business relationships included), and lunch provides a great opportunity for the casual conversation that helps you discover interests you share with others.

How can you tell if you've had a great lunch? It's a good indication that you had a successful business lunch when your client gives you a sincere handshake, or even a hug, as you part company with one another. Things are going well when they say, "Let's do this again soon," and you know they mean it. You also know it's been a successful lunch when you come away having *learned* information about what your client is looking for, and what his or her specific needs are—professionally and, to some extent, personally.

I took my friend Michele out to lunch a few years ago. As the vice president of public relations at a Las Vegas resort, it was very hard for her to get away from work, but she finally made it happen. We had such a great time catching up and being able to talk without interruption.

Michele had a lot going on in her life at the time, and it was great to have the chance to talk with her about it all. As we were wrapping things up, she took my hand and said, "Let's do this at least once a month." This kind of heartfelt behavior can be a good indication that lunch was a success.

I knew I had a knack for making my clients feel good when I invited them to lunch and they started offering to pick up the check! (Of course I would not allow that.) Time will tell, too, if you have had a great lunch with a client.

I wish I had time to share all of the stories I've heard of great ideas and businesses being created when like-minded people shared a great lunch. For example, my cousin, Jodi, is in the business of selling dental supplies. She loves her work and is genuinely interested in the field of dentistry. She was at lunch with one of her clients—a dentist who had been losing business. He shared with her that he was experiencing big decreases in revenue, but that he was certain it wasn't just a case of "losing business to competition." Even though the laws had changed recently in Nevada (which created a huge influx of dentists to the state), he was certain this was not the cause of his losses.

He told her he *wished* he had someone who could "shop" his practice, and tell him what he was doing wrong. Was it something he had done? Was it his front-office staff? What was it about the experience that kept his patients from returning?

When Jodi left the luncheon, her mind began working on the problem. She knew that there were shopping

Power Lunch!

services for retail businesses, but no one had come up with one for medical practices. She came up the idea to start Examine Your Practice, the first service that doctors and medical practitioners could use to find out what their patients were experiencing.

She now offers her service to all kinds of doctors— even veterinarians! How's *that* for a successful lunch? A business lunch can be a master-mind group of synergistic thinking! Two heads are better than one!

Jodi's story is just one of the many I have heard about great businesses and ideas coming from the relaxed setting of lunch with associates. Getting to share ideas with your colleagues can lead to boundless benefits.

Barbara Drazga also experienced an "aha" moment during a business lunch. One of her lunch partners at a seminar started explaining how to choose and order a red wine. She always carries an MP3 recorder and microphone on her, to record impromptu speeches she gives, so she whipped it out and stuck the microphone on her lunch partner's collar—asking him to start at the beginning.

Her guest explained how he acquired the knowledge— it turned out that his father had a vineyard. He went on to explain the etiquette of choosing and testing wine, as well as the complexities of drinking it. They had the recording transcribed and created a quick e-book designed for men who want to impress their dates by knowing the elegant and proper way to choose a wine. Again, two heads thinking along the same lines were able to seize an opportunity that was generated during a business lunch.

Lunch is also a great opportunity to make your guests feel special. What are some of the best ways to accomplish this? Though everyone likes to hear occasional flattery, it is usually obvious when someone is "piling it on." There is a much better way to make people feel special.

One of the very best ways is by *listening* to people. Ask questions and listen to the responses. Rather than initially sharing *your* knowledge about your industry or product with someone else, find out what *they* are looking for, what *they* want, and what *they* need to accomplish. You will be better able to connect with someone emotionally and professionally if you understand what his or her needs are, and where he or she is coming from. Establish a relationship with someone *before* you try to conduct business with them!

Think about it—when was the last time someone asked you about your business needs and actually listened to the answer? If this has happened to you, think back and remember how it made you feel. When someone strives to understand what your needs are, they can better service you or your account, and you can begin to effectively communicate with each other. You really can't help your clients—or sell them anything—if you don't fully understand their needs.

I was at a gaming conference many years ago when an executive from Trump's Taj Mahal in New Jersey took the stage. He spoke about how much they were able to learn from focus groups. He admitted that sometimes executives lose sight of the real bottom line: what their customers want to experience.

The executives had been considering different types of interactive slots, more interesting slot machines, and various new games to attract and retain their customers. They invited some slot players into a special room for a few free rolls of nickels, and some coffee and donuts, in exchange for some answers. They *asked* the customers what would improve their gaming experience.

The executives were floored when the overwhelming answer they received had nothing at all to do with the *types* of games the casinos offered. The answer to what the customers wanted to improve the gaming experience? A *chair* in front of each machine! Those focus groups literally changed the face of slot machine gaming!

When I first moved to Las Vegas, the average casino had a few stools spread throughout the gaming area. The live gaming tables had seats, but the machines did not. You were lucky if you could find a vacant stool and drag it over to your machine. Why? Because few executives ever stood in front of a slot machine for an hour. How could they know how uncomfortable it was?

Boy, have things changed! Now, when you walk into *any* casino, there are chairs physically attached to each slot machine. Players can sit comfortably and gamble for hours—just like at a poker game in their own homes. Can you imagine standing up to play poker for three hours? You would never even consider it! The recent popularity of video poker machines would never have taken off if players had to stand to play. All of this "progress" happened because casino executives were sharp enough to listen to what their customers wanted, and then implement a solution.

Developing effective listening skills will also help you succeed even beyond your business relationships.

Harvey Mackay, author of *The New York Times* best-seller *Swim With the Sharks Without Being Eaten Alive* (Ballantine Books, 1996), believes that: "Lunch and breakfast are still the drive-in windows of opportunity. Make deals, learn the lowdown, and—most of all—build networks." He agrees on the importance of effective listening and reminds us that "the most important input is not what goes into your mouth. It's what goes into your ears. Debrief yourself after a lunch and make private notes. What competitive information did you learn? Take it in, put it down, and—when it makes sense—share what you learn with others who may need to know."

Ask your friends or clients for their advice, and listen to their answers. If you can actually incorporate any advice that they have given you, and follow up later to thank them for their help, you will have taken that relationship to a new level. Such an exchange of ideas and thoughts will demonstrate that you respect their opinions and that you care what they think—just as in business.

I have been able to become friends with most of my clients. I have gotten to the point where I genuinely value their opinions and ideas, as they do mine. We can feel that mutual respect. We often call each other to follow up on things we've discussed. This kind of sharing is a strong dynamic in any relationship. Now we are all caring about each other, and the genuine kindness and concern comes through.

I'm not saying that if a client or a friend gives you advice that you don't agree with that you should run right out and do as he or she advises. But hearing someone else's opinion on something that is going on in your life is always helpful. Weigh the pros and cons of his or her well-intentioned advice, and proceed accordingly. If clients ever help you with a decision, let them know it. (And one of the best ways to thank them is by taking them out for a special lunch, of course!)

I love to give advice and share my opinions. Sometimes my advice is witty and offered in jest. But at other times, in more serious situations, people appreciate a good ear and thoughtful advice. Often, it's just a matter of listening.

I can remember going to my mother on occasion with a problem for which she didn't have the answer, and I also remember how frustrated she would get. I would tell her she didn't need to have the answer, I just needed someone to listen to me. We can often work out our problems for ourselves if we have the help of a sounding board. Now, when I go to her with a situation that might be troubling me, she is more relaxed because she knows that I'm not expecting her to solve my problems. And, often enough, I can come up with the answers I need just from talking with her.

Our clients aren't much different from our mothers, fathers, children, or friends. We all need someone to listen to us. Become a person in your client's life who is always there to lend an ear, and you'll be surprised how much he or she will come to count on you.

Many people are unhappy about their jobs or careers. In those cases, listening and asking questions is the very best response, rather than suggesting definitive action for them to take. Questions pull, and statements push, and you will soon learn that asking some simple questions will open up a whole new aspect to your relationships with your clients.

I have a client who has followed her boss around to three different jobs over the past 15 years. Each move came about because the hotel/casino property where they worked was sold. This past year she thought she might be getting "forced out" of her current position (she had already reached retirement age, and concluded there might be a connection between her advanced age and her deteriorating job situation). In addition, her boss was worried about his own job, and so he didn't feel completely comfortable going to bat for her. She felt betrayed by him, especially after having been with him for so long. (Fear had likely entered the picture, as well, because finding another job was difficult considering her age. Being abandoned or betrayed is never an easy thing to accept. But when you are in your thirties, it is a lot easier to take than when you are 65-plus!) So, I took her to lunch.

While we were dining, she vented about her situation. She was not just feeling angry toward her boss, but also toward the company where they worked. It was easy to sympathize with her when I learned that she had been at that particular company for the longest period of time in her career—more than 11 years!

I didn't say much that day—I mostly listened. But by asking certain questions, I was able to help her realize what she was really angry about. In my friend's case, the "who" and the "why" of her situation were the focal points, because her boss (and friend) had not defended her. She didn't understand why he wouldn't step up to protect her. But when I asked her to think about *why* he wouldn't, I helped her to realize that he was fearful of losing his own job. Once that came to light, we tapped into her compassion and understanding for him (and his family), and that ultimately enabled her to continue working for him once the corporate dust settled. (She is still employed by the same company, and I believe that her boss probably did go to bat for her at some point.)

Remember that basic questions make the best stories. Ask questions related to the *who*, *what*, *when*, *where*, and *why*. This method will help you get to the heart of any matter, and will help you to present yourself as sincerely interested in your client's story. The best part of becoming a good listener is that you will actually become interested in the story—*any* story! You will also find that your work will become more exciting, as you become involved in your client's lives. And, most importantly, when you come home at the end of the day you won't feel as exhausted as you might have before. Being there for others will recharge your own energy reserves.

Always try to help your clients feel good about their jobs, too. That can be as simple as sharing stories about how hard other people have it at their jobs! There is nothing like a true comparison to make someone realize that the grass is *not* always greener on the other side. I'm not advocating that you encourage someone to stay at a job where he or she is miserable. I'm talking about the day-to-day grumblings about dealing with work, stress, or frustration. If you are having lunch with someone who is really unhappy about his or her job, ask questions about what he or she would rather be doing, what he or she is qualified to do, and whether such positions are available.

Most people don't have a "plan B" waiting in the wings. They haven't really thought about what they would rather be doing, or odds are that they would be doing it. Usually their fantasy job is doing what they are currently doing, except for someone else (a bigger company, a smaller company, nicer people, smarter people, and so on), or somewhere they would get a better salary for doing what they do now.

So, your questions can become more focused: "Where would you rather be working?" "Are they hiring?" "Do you know anyone there who is happy?" This is a great example of how to build your relationship with a client or prospect. Anyone can get in his or her face and say, "Yes, quit! They don't deserve you. You'll find something better." But only someone who is truly looking out for their client's best interest would ask what hr or she is *really* looking for, and what he or she is truly hoping to accomplish.

In his book, *The Pursuit of WOW!* (Vintage, 1994), Tom Peters urges his readers to never "waste a single lunch." He explains his reasoning with a personal anecdote: "When I was at McKinsey & Co. in San Francisco, our boss used to get down on bended knee and beg us not to waste lunches eating alone. We were buried in our analyses, and they were important. On the other hand, market development is as much a lunchtime activity as an analytic one. Think about it," he continues, "49 working weeks a year, subtract a few holidays—225 midday opportunities to develop relationships. (Or 450: Power-breakfasting is clearly a growth market.) Even if it means Maalox, Mylanta, or an extra trip to the gym, don't waste those meal slots."

Tom Peters's boss was right. When you know for a fact that taking your clients out and treating them right will elevate your relationships with them, how can you justify eating alone?

Developing a trusting, loyal relationship with your client creates an intimacy usually reserved for friends. Even if you don't begin to socialize with your clients and cross that client/friend line, they will know that you are someone they can trust and in whom they can confide.

This step in building relationships is why there is such a big fuss about business lunches. A successful lunch meeting can not only launch new ventures, but can also cement the building blocks of friendships and relationships that will last long after you and your client have changed jobs, changed careers, or even retired. Learn the secrets to building relationships, and you are on your way to success!

Chapter 2

Appearances:
What You See Is
What You Get

*Unless you're the client,
"Casual Friday" has
no place at a business
lunch.*

Your overall appearance (including how you dress) should be one of your first considerations when planning a business lunch. Being a business professional, you likely check your schedule for the next day and will note that you have a business lunch booked. (Of course, once you learn how much you can accomplish with a business lunch, you should have one booked *every* day!) You will want to make sure that you are dressed appropriately for all of your business lunches.

Casual Friday: A recipe for disaster

I can't stress enough the perils of participating in "casual Friday." It's a great idea for office workers, but if your work takes you outside the office, you need to always dress professionally. Presenting the right appearance will make a huge difference in how you are perceived by your clients.

A dear friend of mine, Pat McRight, was working at KKLZ-FM when she found an article from the Radio Advertising Bureau that should scare any professional enough to keep him or her from taking part in "casual Friday."

According to Pat, the article stated that a good sales rep did away with "casual" days on his own, because one Friday, a friend of his from the local bank called and asked the rep if he could stop by the bank to discuss a proposal.

When the rep arrived, he was ushered into the conference room to find the *whole board of directors of the bank*—in suits and ties! And there he was, in a golf shirt and khakis. The rep could tell by the way the board looked at him that he was at a disadvantage from the moment he walked into the room! He vowed that this would *never* happen again!

Why wouldn't you want to be prepared for an impromptu meeting? I know many associates who have made a mad dash to the mall to buy something for a last-minute, unexpected meeting, when they didn't have time to go home. And women with runs in their stockings are another story! Keep a spare pair in your car, or even in your briefcase. When it comes to ruining a pair of stockings, it is not a question of *if* you are going to ruin them—just a matter of *when*. Why risk having to find just the right outfit, a clean tie, or new stockings, when you have a closet full of options at home?

Make a list of everything you might need for a meeting, and have those items handy (either in your office, or in your car). Women should keep a spare pair of stockings, a toothbrush, neutral undergarments, a curling iron (or other hair "remedy"), a clean blouse, a dress, a jacket, some good, clean generic shoes (black or tan pumps), a scarf, and some makeup (if you wear it). Men should also have an extra sport coat, a toothbrush, a pair of generic shoes (clean loafers), a pair of trousers, a clean shirt, and, especially, a clean tie.

Clean out your closet at home and find some clothing that you don't wear anymore and therefore won't be likely to miss once it's gone. Even if you don't want to participate in casual Friday, you'll feel like a genius the next time you ruin what you are wearing—whether it was a result of having to fix a flat tire, or because you got caught in the rain—and you have a backup ready! Try for classic fashion that doesn't go out of style. If the clothes you chose for your backup are not as trendy as you usually wear, just remember that no one will notice that you are wearing last year's fashions, but they *will* notice that big stain on your shirt or slacks!

When you're hot, you're hot!

If you don't have any meetings scheduled when your day begins, and you really don't think you're going to see anyone that day, you might try to convince yourself that it's okay to dress casually. But no matter *where* you live—whether in a tropical, hot climate, or the freezing north—be prepared!

If you live where the climate is warmer, keep a sport coat or a jacket in your car or office. If you live in a cold climate, keep something dressy at hand, because warm, comfortable clothing tends to be extremely casual.

In the desert, where I live, the temperature can reach the low 100s during the summer. You can blister your hand on the door handle just trying to get into your car. Then, when you sit down inside, you can lose the skin on your thighs if you are wearing a skirt! (The temperature inside a car during a Las Vegas summer can reach upwards of 180 degrees!)

Because of the heat, many salesmen in Las Vegas have adopted golf shirts and slacks as their standard business attire, even though it may not be Friday. The same is true

Wow! Shirley must really need to close that sale.

for salesmen in Hawaii, who can usually be found in big, loose, colorful rayon shirts. But I have seen men in Las Vegas (usually on the selling or agency side), get out of their cars in suits, despite the heat! You know just by looking at them that they must have an important meeting that day. Those are the successful men.

In the summer, ladies can handle the heat by wearing conservative sundresses or separates. I used to wear suits with wonderful silk blouses and stockings, until I started to feel that I looked (and felt) like a mop by 3 p.m.! Would you really want to have a meeting with someone who looked as though she had just been running in her silk suit? A much better option is a simple, lightweight dress that can resist that "slept-in" look. There are exceptions to this of course. I happen to know that one of my clients thinks it is inappropriate to go sleeveless at work. And she is of a mindset that I am not going to change. So, whenever I am planning to see her, I make sure I have a jacket available. This is a "no-brainer." Know your clients, and their preferences. As much as I hate to encourage conformity of any kind, as a seasoned professional, you need to conform to your client's standards if you intend to relate to them on their level.

This rule holds true regardless of your climate. In a colder climate, with snow, rain, sleet, and wind, you will still want to be considerate of how you appear to your clients. Do you really want to show up in galoshes, tracking salt and slush into their offices?

I still remember my time spent working in Cleveland, Ohio (and my hat is off to anyone who deals with the harsh winters). Between the freezing snow and the wind, I often wonder how people can even get out of bed in the morning! You have every right to stay warm, but stop in the restroom on your way to see your clients, and make sure you're presentable.

Take a good, long look at yourself in a full-length mirror before you leave your home. If the reflection you see says, "Here is a qualified business professional," then proceed confidently. If anything about your reflection suggests that you don't care enough, go back to your closet and change. You'll be surprised how much more respect you will earn by looking the part.

There is help available

If you really have trouble putting together outfits, I suggest you enlist some help. Select an associate where you work who has a look you'd like to emulate, and ask him or her to go shopping with you. Most people will appreciate your admiration, and you'll find them eager to help you pull together some outfits, or help you to accessorize your suits. Not everyone has a knack for style, so if you feel you need help in that category, get it!

Another way to put together a more professional wardrobe is to shop for your wardrobe basics at a higher-end store. Most major department stores have an associate called a "personal shopper," whose only job is to help you shop. These people are style experts, who are up on all of the latest trends and fashions. They also know every piece of merchandise that a store carries, so they can save you a lot of time and trouble.

Once you have met a store's personal shopper, shopping can be as simple as calling and telling him or her that you need some new suits or outfits for business. He or she usually prefers to set an appointment so that he or she can give you undivided attention—which will work out better for you, too. When you arrive at the store, he or she will have selected several wardrobe options for you, from suits to shirts, dresses to accessories—even shoes! The personal shopper will also keep a record of your sizes and your preferences.

Most people are surprised to learn that there is usually no additional charge for the services of a personal shopper (they are generally commissioned salespeople, just as the rest of the store's employees are). The convenience and ease of taking advantage of a personal shopper will spoil you for life. The only downside is that you will probably spend a little more because you will love all of his or her suggestions!

If your budget dictates that you shop at discount stores (and you think you need help), don't despair. In this case, find a friend who has great taste and loves to shop. I recently came across a spectacular sweater that was selling for $194.00 at a specialty store. The exact same designer sweater was at a discount store for just $24.95! Unfortunately, it wasn't my size, or I would have snatched it right up! But that is just an example of what you can find if you spend a little time looking through the racks at some of the better discount stores.

Details

Every December in Las Vegas, the National Finals Rodeo comes to town for 10 days. We love our guests and want to make them feel welcome, so the whole town sports Wranglers and Stetsons. Even some of the elite strip hotel/casinos encourage their casino dealers to wear western style clothes. You'll see taxicab drivers in cowboy hats and cocktail waitresses wearing cowboy boots. The usual piped-in Muzak is transformed into country music by artists such as Toby Keith and Wynonna Judd. It's a special time in Las Vegas, and there are no apologies necessary for showing up at a business meeting looking as if your horse might be tied up outside. It's a very colorful time of the year, with the holidays are right around the corner, and the business mood in general is more relaxed.

On the other hand, holidays such as Halloween don't fit into the business environment as easily. Can you imagine trying to negotiate with a client when you're dressed as a pirate, or a fairy princess?

When I worked at a television station, one of our account executives came to work on Halloween dressed as a princess—complete with a plastic mask! That day, she got into a heated argument with our boss regarding a contract.

They were right outside my office, and it was the most surreal argument I've ever witnessed! He was in a business suit, and she was in a floor-length polyester gown with the mask pushed up onto the top of her head. There they stood, toe-to-toe, screaming at each other. Do you think there was any chance she could have explained herself sufficiently (dressed as she was) to win that argument?

Remember to see what your day includes before you leave your home in the morning. If you are ever in doubt about an outfit, don't wear it. Stick to a look that you *know* will be acceptable. You can always dress up later on your own time.

Also remember that your clients can dress in any style they like. They can be in jeans, a three-piece suit, or even a bathing suit (if they are on their way to the beach after your meeting). Your clients are not there to impress you—you are there to impress them. I've had clients apologize for participating in casual Friday, when they showed up for lunch in jeans or shorts. I've just told them how great it was that they got to be comfortable, and not to worry about appearing too casual. My job, and yours, is to put them at ease and make them feel comfortable. That means you must totally accept them as they are.

Fragrance

I know the following can be hard advice to accept (because you will always want to smell clean and fresh), but go easy on the fragrance. If you have ever eaten in a restaurant where the hostess walked by your table and for a moment you thought you were eating at the fragrance counter at Saks Fifth Avenue, then you'll know how offensive a heavy fragrance can be. Try to remember that not everyone shares your love of scents, so go lightly—or even skip it for business lunches.

For men, it's not as great a problem, in that a light aftershave lotion will likely have dissipated by lunchtime.

However, many women like to freshen up before lunch. They go off to the ladies room, where they touch up their makeup, respray their hair, slather on hand cream, and finish with a blast of cologne. (Then I get to pick them up and drive them to lunch, knowing I will practically need an allergy pill beforehand! Because they are my clients, I don't say a word. But if our roles were reversed, I would hate to put off a client because I had overdone it with beauty products before our meeting.) Regardless of whether or not you enjoy strong smells and fragrances, you should always be considerate when preparing for your business day—especially if you have a business meeting— and use fragrance as though you *know* it will bother your client. And remember: Smelling "soap and water clean" is always your best bet!

Send the right message

Finally, and particularly for the ladies, keep in mind that the appearance you present can help you to send the right message. If your manner of dress is too revealing, you may find that your clients will get the wrong impression about you, in spite of your professional behavior.

Wearing a low-cut neckline, a short skirt or dress, or some other provocative outfit sends the wrong message completely. You don't have to give up style—or even your femininity—to dress for success. But if you wear loud, slinky, or sexy clothes to work, you may be asking for trouble. I recently read that even casual Fridays have gotten out of hand in offices across the country, because some women are wearing low-cut jeans and midriff tops, revealing pierced belly-buttons and tattoos. This look has no place in the business world (unless you are working for a clothing manufacturer who creates that kind of look). I'd rather see someone err on the side of being too conservative, rather than too sexy or casual.

Men need to be aware that business fashion for ladies often crosses the lines. Just because someone you are working with looks sexy, it doesn't mean she wants to start something with you! Education of interpersonal skills in business has come a long way since the 1960s, as sexual harassment suits started springing up in response to the force of women's rights. Now, corporations teach "diversity in the workplace" and "sexual harassment education," along with actual job and management training.

Men and women need to respect each other as individuals. I once heard a friend talking about her "Secret Weapon." I asked her what she was talking about, and she shared her story with me. As you read this, you may find it hard to believe that anyone in business today, especially her male boss, would have so little regard for someone as a human being, let alone the lack of respect for his clients. Here's the story of the "Secret Weapon":

> Though employed as strictly a "numbers" person, my former supervisor often liked to take advantage of my other, um, assets ("The Secret Weapon"), to navigate through any delicate business lunch with thorny clients. The Secret Weapon was often employed to manipulate an exigent deal back on the favor of "our side" or to persuade a revenue-challenged client to get on an automatic payment plan. Under the perverted theory that men can and often will be distracted by an attractive woman (or even an ugly one with large breasts), the idea is to establish the lunch as a social outing

complete with flirtatious and witty repartee, whereby the "difficult ones" are so charmed by the Secret Weapon, that when the talk actually does come around to the business at hand, the X chromosomes have already been so charmed by the Ys that it is significantly easier to attain the desirable outcome of the meeting. "It's like taking candy from a baby," my boss would say. Predictably, the Secret Weapon got the win nearly every time.

Incredible as it may seem, this tactic worked! Are men led that easily? Are women that easy to take advantage of? Are bosses unaware of the position they put a female employee in when they say, "I need you to break out the 'Secret Weapon' at lunch tomorrow, so dress appropriately"? I'm sure a sharp lawyer would love to have a crack at her boss in a courtroom!

Deciding who to feel sorry for was a tough choice—my friend, or the clients. Either way, it was an incredible story that illustrates the worst in all of us. I hope, as we move into a more enlightened age of doing business, the people who have operated this way realize the error of their ways!

Chapter 3

First Meetings: The Business "Date"

Avoid an awkward first meeting by picking up your clients at their office.

Whether you are male or female, and whether your client is male or female, creating business relationships can sometimes be as awkward as dating. You probably know a few people who don't actively date because they are afraid of being "shot down" when asking someone out. Well, that's a luxury you can't afford in business. You must be willing to take the initiative, and dive right in.

Put yourself in your client's position. He or she is at his or her office, with plenty of work to do. They have dozens of friends and associates with whom they can book a lunch date. Why, then, should they take the time to meet you—someone new who is most likely trying to sell them something? And aside from his or her conscientious desire to learn about you, your product, services, or something that *may* benefit his or her company or business, he or she may be filled with dread at the thought of having to get through a lunch with a stranger. There are not a lot of good reasons that he or she should let down his or her guard and go with you—that is, unless you *give* him or her a reason or two!

The odds are that your prospects feel you need them more than they need you. It's up to you to prove otherwise. Your job is to become valuable to them in any way you can. But before you impress them, you have to meet them! So how do you get a new client to meet you, and, eventually, have lunch with you?

The first steps

There are four great ways to meet new clients:

1. Introductions.

2. Networking.

3. Offering needed information or services.

4. The "Loving Mother Method of Sales."

Introductions

The first (and best) way to meet new people, potential customers, and clients is to have a mutual friend introduce you to each other. When Napoleon Hill accepted Andrew Carnegie's proposal to define and record the "secret formula" for success by interviewing the world's richest men, he offered no compensation to them—only a letter of introduction from Mr. Carnegie himself. As Hill interviewed these leaders of industry, he quickly learned the value of an introduction. Owners of large corporations and small businesses alike, along with other self-made men, were eager to share their experiences with Hill simply because he had a letter of introduction from Andrew Carnegie.

If you don't have an associate who can make an introduction for you, there are other ways of getting to see someone. Start by trying to learn as much as possible about your client. In our wonderful Internet age, search engines are extremely helpful for this. You may even be able to go through his or her assistant to learn some valuable information. Assistants and secretaries aren't usually as defensive as their bosses can be when it comes to letting new people near. Sometimes, however, a secretary or assistant can be even tougher to get past. My friend A.J. told me she recently heard of a receptionist referred to by the term "Rejectionist," because it was this staff member who decided which calls got through to the decision-makers, and which ones didn't! If you ever encounter a "rejectionist," use the Loving Mother Method of Sales (which I explain later in this chapter), and make that person your first priority.

The more people you know, the greater your chances are that you will know someone who is acquainted with the person you would like to meet. Ask around, and, if you find that mutual acquaintance, invite him or her to bring your prospect to a special luncheon so that you can meet him or her. This is quite possibly the bestcase scenario. You should have a fabulous meeting and be able to take it from there with some good follow-up.

Similarly, don't forget about your other clients. There's a good chance that you could get "grandfathered in" to a new account with the help of one of your existing clients. If you have a hard time getting in to see someone, it's possible that one of your other clients may know that person (and would be willing to make a call on your behalf). Sometimes, just knowing that you're okay in someone else's book will be enough to turn the key for you. And executives usually appreciate getting closer to others in their field, in case they ever need to make a move. Getting a good client to hook you up with a prospect is a wonderful experience. If you have a client who does this for you, make sure you thank him or her with a special gift.

Networking

Networking functions are another wonderful way to meet the people you want to know. A friend of mine, who recently became president of his own company, told me that now that his business, and its subsequent success, are his direct responsibility, he networks more actively than when he worked for another company! This is an educated, hardworking professional, and he had to admit to *himself* that he hadn't been taking full advantage of all of the networking opportunities he had in the past. Now, he makes sure to "work the room" for all it's worth.

I think most of us have a tendency to gravitate toward the people we know when attending a breakfast, luncheon, or other networking event. Let's face it: We don't get to see enough of the people we like, and these events offer the perfect opportunity to get caught up with each other, listen to a guest speaker, and leave with a little more than what we came with. But, if your net worth depends on building your circle of friends and associates, you should work those rooms as though your life depends on it! If there was a prize of $10,000 for the person who collected the most business cards at a mixer, you'd probably break your leg trying to win, wouldn't you? Now think about this: Meeting the right person at a networking event could, literally, mean $10,000 in your pocket—if you build a relationship with the person who leads to business (which leads to subsequent sales and referrals). In fact, this type of networking could lead to millions of dollars in your pocket, if you meet the right person. Still want to sit and visit with your friends?

You should walk around the room with your business cards within easy reach and talk to everyone you can. Develop a strong and sincere sound bite (or introduction) that will get your message across in 30 seconds or less. The purpose of a sound bite is to briefly introduce yourself, explain who you are, and what you do. It's a great way to find common ground or mutual associates.

I usually say, "Hi. I'm Robin Jay, and I'm an author and public speaker. I wrote *The Art of the Business Lunch: Building Relationships Between 12 and 2*. I teach people the importance of breaking bread with their clients as a way of building relationships, and how to take those relationships to a higher level." If the person I am addressing shows interest, I can delve into more detail. Then I make sure to ask who he or she is and what he or she does in return. They usually respond similarly to how I addressed them, offering who they are and what they do. I always ask for their business card, and offer them one of mine. If there is something I need to remember about that person, I will make a note on the back of his or her card. The more people I meet, the more friendships I can create. The more relationships I build, the more success I can achieve. The greater my circle of acquaintances becomes, the better my chances are of knowing someone who can introduce me to other people I want to know.

Volunteer at your networking functions, too. The more organizations you belong to, the greater your circle of influence will become. If there is an organization that specifically caters to your client's industry, I recommend that you join that organization first. In helping others, you will ultimately end up helping yourself. Whether you belong to your local chamber of commerce, or an industry-specific organization, you will reap untold benefits in exchange for your service.

When I was selling advertising, I liked to attend the breakfasts hosted by the Nevada Development Authority (NDA), a nonprofit organization that works to help businesses relocate to Nevada. These breakfasts feature *all* of the new businesses that are coming to our area. There are special, reserved tables for the newest members, and the president of the NDA walks around with a microphone so that each new member can announce who they are, what his or her company does, and other pertinent information. It is new business for anyone in the room, served up on a silver platter!

(If you are uncomfortable at networking events, I'll offer some additional suggestions in Chapter 15.)

Offering Needed Information or Services

Looking for ways to be of service to your prospects, and then following through, is another great way to begin to build a relationship with them. I always know that once I can get a prospect out to lunch, I can earn his or her trust and business. I can usually get a head start on that by showing up at his or her office and providing him or her with valuable information.

When I worked for Highway Radio (KHWY), we always had the latest visitor statistics for Las Vegas, as related to the drive-up tourist market from California. (The highway station broadcasts a signal from several transmitters along Interstate 15, so that you can pick up the station for the entire four- to five-hour drive from California.) That route is responsible for more than 40 percent of all Las Vegas tourism. My clients were always grateful to have these boring Department of Transportation statistics compiled in a neat, easy-to-read format. Our company's owner and president, Howard Anderson, knew the value of having a reason to stop by to visit his prospects, as well as the value of providing our clients with information that would help them to do their jobs more effectively. Companies and individuals should always think of creating valuable re-search for their clients—not just as a practical "foot-in-the-door" opportunity, but also in an effort to provide service to their clients.

As the years passed, the traffic counts climbed but re-mained "evergreen." Where they had been high, they con-tinued to be high, and where they were low, they continued to be low. Only the overall volume increased. The fairly boring statistics were growing even more boring. That's when we began conducting psychographic and demo-graphic research on the "highway visitors," by conduct-ing intercept studies. The published results of these studies gave our clients an even better source of information about *their* clients—information that no one else could provide them with! KHWY was exemplary in its effort to become invaluable to its clients—and this made our jobs that much easier. I don't recall a time when dropping off our statis-tics and research didn't help me to succeed in getting through to my prospects.

Think about how you can better service your clients, or provide them with the information they need, and you will find an open path to their door.

The "Loving Mother Method of Sales"

We've all heard stories about, or experienced first-hand, mothers who want you to eat, eat, eat. Well, believe it or not, one of the ways I have found tremendous success in getting clients out to lunch is by stopping by with doughnuts, bagels, or other treats.

Showing up at an office with midmorning snacks is a great way to get your foot in the door. No one is likely to give you the boot when your arms are full of warm bags of fresh pastries. I don't think I've ever had to deliver doughnuts more than twice before I succeeded in booking a lunch date with a client. (Note: If you discover your client is on a low-carb diet, or has some other food preferences, make sure you don't show up with doughnuts. Instead, bring something appropriate—fresh veggies, fruit, cheeses, and so on). You will only be limited by your creativity. I have even stopped by an office with a cooler full of ice cream when it was 110 degrees outside.

In most instances, a call to your client's office will have his or her secretary revealing your prospect's weakness or preferences (secretaries will know that he or she, too, will get some type of treat, and will appreciate your checking with him or her). It's not that anyone will reveal corporate secrets for a doughnut or a cookie. Rather, it's similar to visiting a friend's home—you would never stop by empty-handed. When you call first, you will also find out if your client is going to be in that day. If your client is out and you still stop by to visit with everyone in the office (including a "rejectionist!"), you will always score big points with them, *and* learn a lot!

If your client is there, but is in a meeting (or otherwise unable to see you), you can still accomplish a lot. There's no such thing as a wasted visit. Aside from showing up with treats (and hopefully getting everyone in a better mood), you might even be able to learn *more* by visiting with the office staff than you would by speaking to your client directly. Go on a fact-finding mission. If you pay attention to what is going on in the office, you will learn many valuable things. Just some of what I have learned or received through visiting has included:

- ⏰ Personal information about my clients, such as when and where they were planning to vacation, the fact that they were moving into a new house, just got a puppy, and so on.

- ⏰ My client's business card, which often includes his or her direct phone number and e-mail address.

- ⏰ A glimpse of his or her office, which can reveal the client's favorite sports teams, favorite recreational activities, and other preferences.

- ⏰ The mood of the office (whether everyone is happy to be there, or if you could cut the tension with a knife).

Anything I learn or observe can help me to establish a new relationship with a client.

So, what do you do with this information? All of this knowledge provides you with an opening for a follow-up note, a gift, or an opportunity to do something special for them. If you found out your client couldn't see you because he or she was rushing to get everything done before leaving on a vacation, you might offer a contact in the location he or she is visitng—whether it's the name of a great restaurant, or a special value of which he or she could take advantage. If you found out he or she just got a puppy, you could drop off a $25 gift card (or more, considering the value of your client) for the local pet supply store. And, if he or she is moving into a new house, you could prepare a list of your favorite interior designer, landscaper, housekeeper, handyman, or other specialist whose services might be needed.

Just get creative. It doesn't have to cost you a lot to service your clients or prospects. It is just a great way to show that you care about them and that you have their best interest at heart. When Bob Walsh became the marketing director at the Sahara Hotel and Casino, I found out that he was from Cleveland and had attended St. Edward's Catholic School for Boys in Lakewood, Ohio (a suburb of Cleveland). A week later, while visiting my family in Cleveland, I found a framed print of "St. Ed's" and purchased it for my client. Can you imagine how thrilled he was when I presented it to him? I'm sure I was his only rep who knew where he went to school. Now, everyone knows—because they've seen the print! He loved talking to me about growing up in Cleveland, and we have remained good friends ever since.

Each of these bits of information or knowledge can be gained simply by learning to think as a caring, nurturing parent. Take good care of your people, and have their best interests at heart, and they will soon learn that you are on *their* side.

One more way to get a great lunch date and build your business relationships, though not with "new" clients, is by going through your older accounts.

I once attended a networking luncheon with Michael Bushendorf, from Outdoor Promotions, and he told me how he had called some of his former clients (who hadn't bought advertising from him for several months). He explained how he invited each of these former clients to lunch. He said that during the lunches they talked about business—what was going on, and why these particular clients hadn't been buying lately. It turned out that, though each of them had stopped buying for one reason or another, they agreed that it was time to start advertising again. He said that by simply going back through his old accounts, and inviting these clients to lunch, he had regained two major accounts in just one week! So make sure that if you are sitting on a gold mine you remember to work it while pursuing new accounts.

Lastly, I need to mention that you should never forget your sense of humor, especially when you are trying to break down barriers. A good laugh can take you far. LuAnn Terrell, owner of Showtime Marketing, told me that whenever she needed to get in to see someone and found herself in "voice-mail hell," that she would leave a funny message. For example, she might say, "Mr. Johnson, I've left you three voice mails already and I haven't heard back from you yet. Please don't turn me into a stalker!"

This approach may not be for everyone, but LuAnn told me that it invariably worked for her. Her clients would call her back laughing and say, "Well, now, I wouldn't want to do *that* to you. I've just been really busy lately," and so on. Find your own rhythm or "line" that works for you. Persistence, professionalism, kindness, generosity, and a sense of humor will help you to get that first "date."

The "Date"

You may think this is a "no-brainer," but one of the very first things you must know is how to respect the clock. Be on time! My punctual friend Janice told me about a lunch date she had scheduled with the executive senior vice president of what was, at that time, one of the largest gaming companies in the world.

Janice worked for a group of gaming magazines, and this luncheon was set so that she could make a presentation to renew the contract for *all* of the gaming company's properties. She knew this man was very busy and that she would only have a brief sliver of his time. Needless to say, this was a huge meeting.

At the last minute, Janice's publisher called and said he wanted to accompany her to the meeting. She suggested they meet at the client's, but he insisted that she wait for him at their office, so that they could go together. By the time he joined her, and they got to the client's office, they were half an hour late! The client, whose ego rivaled the publisher's, was incensed at being kept waiting. The client told them that he did not have time to eat with them, and that they now had just 10 minutes for the presentation.

Can you imagine what a 45-minute presentation looks like when it's been reduced to 10 minutes? Right after the hurried presentation, the executive senior vice president told my friend and her publisher that he would not be renewing his contract with the magazine. Not being able to renew this account cost Janice more than $60,000 in lost commissions.

What a tragedy to suffer such a huge loss from just *one* client! And that was just *her* commission. Can you even calculate what it must have cost her publisher? I have wondered if he ever kicks himself for making her late to the presentation. Was their tardiness the reason the client refused to renew? Did wasting the client's time put him in such a negative frame of mind that he chose, right at that moment, to cease doing business with them? Only the client knows for sure.

We all know that there can be extenuating circumstances, from traffic jams, to getting lost on your way to an appointment. It is wonderful when your clients understand about such delays. Now that everyone in business is equipped with a cell phone, a simple call can alleviate much of the stress if you find yourself stuck in a traffic jam. Regardless, if you plan on being early to your meetings, you will find that your work will become less stressful, and your clients will always appreciate the fact that you are prompt.

Once you have a lunch date booked with a new acquaintance, you may face some interesting challenges. If your date is with a client that you have not yet met face to face, you will most likely find it can hold the potential to be quite an awkward meeting if you are not prepared. I'm sure this is one reason why blind dates are so stressful! How do you find your new client in a restaurant when you have no idea what he or she looks like? I've gotten so used to first meetings that now it is easy for me to rendezvous with a stranger. I simply look for the most anxious, uncomfortable person in the restaurant's lobby! Seriously, most people are usually uncomfortable about the prospect of meeting someone for the first time. People don't always look the way they sound on the telephone, and it is difficult to recognize someone from just a conversation or two. This is where a reservation and a great restaurant come in handy.

Any sophisticated host or hostess at a higher-end restaurant can make sure that two parties will find each other. Simply tell your client that you have a reservation under your name, and that you will see him or her there. Then, arrive a few minutes early, and make sure the host or hostess knows not just your name, but that you are waiting for your client. Tell the host or hostess your client's name as well.

Etiquette dictates that you should wait for your guest at the hostess desk, which can alleviate the risk of missing each other, but sometimes that area gets crowded, or your guest will be running late. If you are seated and can get some work done at the table while you wait, the client won't feel bad about making you wait, plus you can take advantage of that time to be productive. When you see the host bringing your guest to your table, always stand up (whether you are a man *or* a woman), greet him or her with a friendly handshake, and do your best to put him or her at ease.

Another way to ease the stress of a "blind" meeting with a client is to give a brief description of your appearance when you confirm your lunch date (either directly, or with his or her assistant). For example, I might say, "I'm 5'6", I have long blonde hair worn down, and I'll be wearing an aqua dress." Imagine walking into a restaurant and having a detailed description such as that. How easy would it be to pick me out of a crowd? If you are 5'5" with short brown hair, and are wearing a black suit, you may fit the same description as a few of the other patrons. Because of this, you should try to wear something distinctive for a first meeting.

A man might say, "I'm 6'2", wearing a gray suit with a bright blue tie, and I have short salt-and-pepper hair." If someone is looking for a man who fits that description (which may apply to several men in a restaurant at lunchtime), and they think they've found him in the restaurant, the bright blue tie will be a differentiating factor. Try to make it easy on your clients.

Another clever way to help ease the stress of the situation is to e-mail a photo of yourself to your client on the day you are going to meet. Between cell phone cameras and e-mail, you can easily have someone at your office snap a digital photo of you in what you are wearing *that morning* so that you can then send it to your client. This will make it even easier for him or her to find you. And if you didn't already have your client's e-mail address, it's a great way to get it!

I remember in many old movies men would wear a red carnation in their lapels so they could be identified. You can always resort to an obvious solution such as that, too, except that a flower might be hard to spot in a crowded restaurant.

Though all of these suggestions are helpful for identifying a stranger, try to pick a smaller, less-crowded restaurant for first-time encounters, if possible. Your client will appreciate your thoughtfulness.

The very *best* way, however, to avoid the entire rendezvous drama is to pick up your client at his or her office. Is there anything more simple? You can wait in the lobby of the office (if he or she works for a large company), and have the receptionist let him or her know you are there. Or, upon the client's suggestion, you can just find him or her at his or her desk. Problem solved. You have so much going on with a business lunch, that there is no need to complicate the simpler points. Plus picking your client up at his or her office has other benefits, as I explain in the next chapter.

Chapter 4

Transportation: Getting There Can Be Half the Fun

Drive your client to and
from a business lunch
whenever possible.

"**S**hall I meet you there, or can you pick me up?" I have heard that question for nearly every lunch date I've ever booked. And I have a strong opinion about this: Pick up your client and drive him or her to and from the restaurant whenever possible. The reason? Intimacy. Having a quiet drive with your client in your car can be a great bonding opportunity. Remember that there are some risks (for example, in the case of an accident, you or your company could be held liable), but they are outweighed by the benefits.

One executive told me about a case that had recently been settled in Florida. Driving a client home after a business dinner, a radio station's sales manager's car was hit by a truck. The manager and client had shared a bottle of wine with dinner, although the accident was ruled the fault of the truck driver. The client not only sued the truck driver, he also sued the restaurant for serving the wine, and he sued the radio station where the sales manager worked. It was devastating for the station, its management, and the sales manager who was driving the car that night. The station's new policy is to meet clients at the restaurant.

If you are the president of your own company, you will want to give careful consideration to establishing guidelines for entertaining clients. If you work for a company, you will want to check with your employer to see if your company has a policy pertaining to this. Always pay attention when you're driving, *especially* when you have someone else in your car! That being said, whenever possible you should offer to pick up and drive your client to and from the restaurant.

When I was selling advertising, particularly to the mega resorts in Las Vegas, I knew that a good deal of my clients had to park far away from their offices. It could take someone half of his or her lunch hour just to get to the car and back. I would always suggest that I pick them up, and I would always tell them that it was no problem. I would then go to their office to get them and would give them a call when I was outside if parking was difficult. They would join me and would always thank me profusely for saving them the hassle of taking their own car. Then, back on the road, I would make sure that I was the safest, most defensive driver in the world!

A ride in your car with a client offers privacy that you can't get in a restaurant. People will usually open up and share with you when they know that no one is eavesdropping nearby. Sometimes they will discuss their family, sometimes medical problems, and sometimes they will reveal secrets about their jobs. I have been told about budgets and budget cuts, the competition—both the client's and my own—my client's stock portfolios, extra-marital affairs, and other sensitive information—all while driving to or from lunch. I try hard to forget most of it, especially when it comes to things I wish my clients hadn't shared! But being there, offering an ear, and then keeping a confidence, are well rewarded.

There are many subjects that people like to talk about, but a job change is one of the most sensitive.

People always seem to want to share their biggest decisions with a friend, such as when they are going to make a change, or if they are considering a change. But they would be in jeopardy if their employer were to find out they were looking before they had a chance to resign. I have known of impending changes months before they actually occurred, and trust is gained by keeping a secret. The more trustworthy you become, the more information clients will share with you.

This information may or may not help you in your job, but the relationships you build will always help you. A kept confidence is never forgotten! I served on the board of directors for Las Vegas Women in Communications as job bank director for three years. Building a reputation for helping people to find jobs, and for being able to keep a confidence, has stayed with me. Long after I had taken on a different board position, associates continued to call me for job leads and referrals. And I still love to help people find great jobs.

Always take advantage of the opportunity to pick up your clients and drive them to your lunch meetings whenever possible. Make sure that your car is clean and neat. If you have a child's car seat in the passenger's seat, move it before you pick up your client. If you have fast-food wrappers or spilled soft drink bottles in your car, you may as well forget about making any kind of good impression. You should always keep your car clean regardless of whether or not you are planning on picking up your clients, because plans can always change. (Besides, having a clean car will make you feel better all day, too.)

Separate yourself from the crowd!

Have you ever thought of picking up your clients in a limousine? This is an incredible way to make a grand, lasting impression! Talk about making your client feel special! It may be the only time they will ever get to ride in one. And if they are used to riding in one, then you will succeed in making them comfortable.

If it is a special occasion, such as their birthday or their first day on a new job, give them the red-carpet treatment. Get creative and you will see a real difference in your relationships. For new clients, picking them up in a limo says that you are willing to do anything for them. It shows that you want to impress them, that you are eager to accommodate them, and that you care about making them feel special. Isn't that exactly the message you want to send? Picking up your clients in a limousine lends an air of success to you and your work. You will find that most business professionals want to associate with other successful people. You will certainly get their attention, and whether they are accustomed to the royal treatment or not, they are likely to remember that limo ride with you for a long time.

Most cities have exotic car rental agencies, too. That is an easy, although expensive, way to impress clients and make them feel special. Imagine treating someone to this fantasy: It's the first warm day of spring, especially wonderful because it's been a miserable winter. You arrive to pick up your client in a sporty convertible and let *him or her* drive *you* to lunch! Who wouldn't remember *that* for the rest of their lives? You could even eat lunch at a drive-in, just for the joy of sitting in a car with the top down!

This isn't for everyone, though. I would recommend that you do this for a client you already know, and one that you believe has an affinity for either convertibles, or who enjoys great weather!

If your client is an older male, he might be more impressed with a Mercedes convertible than a Mustang. If your client is a younger male, he might prefer a Porsche. And if you are picking up a female client in an exotic car, make sure it is something that she will feel great in—such as a Mercedes, or Jaguar convertible. Renting an exotic car is a great way to impress your clients, but make sure you are on the right track with your selection. The agency you use can probably help you to decide, or you can fish for ideas when you talk to your client or his or her assistant.

Chapter 5

Choosing the Perfect Restaurant

Always make a

reservation!

Deciding *where* to take a client for your business lunch is more important than you might think, especially when you consider how much is communicated by your choice. If you've ever dined at a restaurant with patio seating near a fountain or a parking lot, then you can imagine what it must be like to try to discuss business at a rock concert! The noise from a fountain will have you shouting your business, and any hope of bonding or intimacy will be lost.

The restaurant you choose reflects not only your character and personality, but also shows your client how much regard you have for them. If it is the first time you are taking a particular client to lunch, play it safe. Choose a restaurant that offers consistent quality, is moderately priced, and, fairly quiet. My first choice would be a restaurant such as The Palm, or The Capital Grille. If you've never been to either of these restaurants, let me describe them for you, as you may know something similar in your city.

These restaurants are perfect for business: The waiters wear clean, white jackets, there is a lot of wood (on the walls, the floor, the booths and the chairs), there are crisp, white tablecloths at lunchtime, and the service is top-notch. Waiters are aware of guests conducting business, and they don't intrude to ask how everything is if it is apparent that things at the table are fine. They also accept reservations (so you know you will have a table waiting for you and your client). The Palm even offers an affordable prix fixe lunch menu. There are no surprises, which is *exactly* what you want for a first-time business lunch.

I recently took a client to a southwestern-style restaurant, and the difference in service between this restaurant and one that I would normally choose for business was staggering. I had suggested taking her to The Palm, because we had a lot of business to discuss, but she insisted on going to this other restaurant because she needed to stay closer to her office. It helped that I had known Cammie for a couple of years, but she had just changed jobs and become my client, so this was our first *business* lunch together.

I had a media kit at the table and was getting her up to date on her account. Our waiter was very nice and friendly, but was oblivious to the fact that we were trying to conduct a business lunch. He interrupted us to inform us of their "exciting happy hour with half-priced appetizers." He also stopped by frequently to ask how everything was going. Later in the meal, he interrupted again—this time to hand us some 3 × 5 cards to fill out to join the restaurant's birthday club! We kept looking at each other through each of his "presentations," and laughed when he had finally left us alone. Thank goodness I am friends with Cammie! If this had been a new client that I didn't know, it could have been incredibly awkward.

You should always give careful consideration to how expensive the restaurant is that you choose. If your client is on a budget at home, and the lunch check for two of you is $80, you might make him or her uncomfortable. On the other hand, if your client is well-off (and he or she spends a great part of his or her budget with you), and you take him or her to an $8.99 buffet, the chances are good that he or she will be offended (or, worse yet, perceive you as cheap). You want to find not just the right price, but the best combination of great service, food quality, and ambiance—*especially* for a first-time meeting.

The "top 10 list of criteria"

I have established a top 10 list of criteria to consider when choosing a restaurant for a business lunch. I believe it is necessary to have *all* of these elements present, particularly for a *first* lunch, or for any business lunch involving a presentation:

1. **Top-notch service.** The right service can make or break a deal. Great service is not an option!

2. **A fabulous menu.** Stay away from the exotic. Instead, offer a great, fresh selection.

3. **The right size room.** Seek out large tables with privacy. For a major presentation, find a restaurant that offers a private room, complete with audio-visual capability.

4. **The right acoustics.** A room that is too loud will have your clients shouting their business, and could make them uncomfortable. Too quiet and they may fear being overheard.

5. **The right price.** Expensive is impressive, but you can go overboard. A restaurant that features a prix fixe business lunch menu is ideal—and is guaranteed to make your boss happy.

6. **A great location.** Stay as close as possible to your client's office. Doing so will give you more time to talk.

7. **Accepts reservations.** Can you imagine meeting your client only to find that the restaurant you chose is booked solid? What a disaster! Make sure they accept reservations, and call ahead.

8. **The right amount of action.** Impress your client with movers and shakers, or even a celebrity sighting!

9. **Accepts credit cards.** *Never*, ever pay for a business lunch with cash!

10. **Consistency.** You have a lot riding on your meetings. It always helps to stack the deck in your favor.

Create your own top 10 list

Create a list of your favorite restaurants that are suitable for business lunches. Organize the list geographically, by community, suburb, or business district.

Take advantage of trying new places when you go to lunch socially with your friends, before you take a client. When you discover a restaurant that is just right for business, you can add it to your list of restaurant options for your business lunches.

Keep this list handy when you confirm your lunch dates so that you don't end up in the twilight zone of indecision with regard to where you are going to meet. We've all been there, asking, "Where are you going to be?," "What do you feel like eating today?," or "Where do you want to go?" By having a list of "perfect" restaurants handy, you will be able to be flexible—yet still in the position to choose a place that will work for business. This also lets you offer suggestions to your client (allowing him or her to choose), while you still maintain control of the destination.

Similarly, you should learn your area as well as possible, so that you will know what is available, depending on where you will be. Sometimes a client needs to stay close to his or her office. They will usually suggest a favorite restaurant in an area near their office. In that case, go with the flow. Remember that you want them to feel comfortable (and if they are suggesting a place that they frequent, this is more likely to be the case).

If there is a specific area where a majority of your clients work, try to frequent the restaurants in that area, so you will have a suggestion handy when one says they need to stay close to the office. If you can surprise them with a great choice near their office (one that they might not have known about), you will be a hero.

I am very fortunate to live in Las Vegas, as it has become a diner's paradise. We thought we were lucky when we got a TGI Friday's back in the 80s. Now the city boasts some of the world's greatest restaurants. We have spectacular views, contemporary themes, and incredible food. Not all of these restaurants are open for lunch, but there are still many wonderful places to choose from. But *every* city across the country has its secret hideaways, fabulous delicatessens, Italian restaurants with checkered tablecloths, and other great options to help you accomplish

85

So…Mr. Johnson, where would you like to have lunch today…Egypt, Paris, or New York??

your business lunch objectives. Get to know the choices, and become an expert. Make sure if a new restaurant opens in your city, you are one of the first people to experience it.

An insider's secret

One of the best ways to discover the great restaurants in your city is to purchase a copy of the Zagat Survey's dining guide for that particular area. It is generally sold at bookstores and is also available online at *www.Zagat.com*. The Zagat readers give their opinions on restaurants, and these are then compiled and edited. The information this service provides is priceless! This is also your best bet for finding great restaurants (and golf courses) when you travel. You can go online to see what cities are served by Zagat, and order a copy for any city you'll be visiting.

You might think you don't need a publication such as Zagat, because wherever you stay you find a great local magazine in your hotel room featuring dining suggestions. These are called "tourist publications," and they cater to their advertisers. You will never read a bad review about a restaurant in such a publication! The editorial reviews are offered only for the magazine's advertising clients, and the magazine would be foolish to criticize their clients.

In the Zagat Survey, however, you will read actual reviews by people who love to dine out. They *will* tell you if a restaurant "needs a face-lift," or if it is "just another cattle call." One gourmet room in Las Vegas earned the following line: "it's an upscale experience that's worth the home equity loan." You won't ever read *that* kind of review in a tourist pub! Good service, price, décor—it's all there in this wonderful, unique dining guide. I can't imagine traveling without a copy of the book for my destination city.

My clients have said that I always pick the best, and newest, places to dine. And they always enjoy the discovery. They have told me they can't wait to bring their spouses or friends back to the new places we've tried. They know that I know good food, and that I want to make our lunch date special, and that has helped me to earn their trust. We look at lunch as an adventure, and we laugh and have the best time experiencing all the exciting, new places together.

Having the confidence that you know where to go, or that you are aware of the latest restaurant opening, will make your clients even more excited about meeting you for lunch.

I get teased a lot (in good fun) for being in the know about the latest hot spots. In fact, I had a client, Sharon, call me once from her hospital bed, where she was recovering from open-heart surgery. She wanted to know if there was a decent restaurant near the hospital in which she was recuperating. She thought she would send her aunt Pam out to get them a great lunch "to go" and bring it back to her hospital room for them to enjoy together. I was the first one she thought of when she needed to know what great restaurants were in the area. I had to laugh at my reputation. That was the first time someone declared me "The Queen of the Business Lunch!"

Making lunchtime special

Keep track of your client's birthdays, or other special occasions, and celebrate accordingly. Let your waiter know that it's your client's birthday and remember to present your guest with a card or special gift once you are seated.

Even a simple remembrance, something professional or something wacky, will show your thoughtfulness and will make them feel special. I can remember such an occasion from more than 10 years ago, when a friend and associate of mine, Pat Miller, who is now a team leader at the Warner Brothers television network, took me out to lunch for my birthday (which falls on Halloween). She gave me a pencil with a big, blood-shot eyeball on the end! It was so hysterically funny and silly. She also got me a card, and bought lunch.

It's that kind of gesture that is so endearing—the fact that she remembered my birthday, and made it fun. Whenever I am out with Pat, I tell our server it's her birthday, so that everyone has to sing to her. She cringes with embarrassment. These are the memories that not only make work more fun, but will make you feel good inside. It's a great feeling to give to others—and giving helps to cement a relationship.

For special occasions, it is all right to take your guest someplace more indulgent than you would otherwise. Most of my guests appreciate the "big deal" that I make over their birthdays. For those lunches, I always choose a restaurant that makes a fuss over a guest's birthday.

As you work to build your list of acceptable restaurants, you might be tempted to try an ethnic restaurant, but be careful. Ethnic restaurants can be wonderful, or they can become your worst nightmare! If your client is a meat-and-potatoes person and you take him or her to your favorite ethnic restaurant, you will not make any points for yourself. You may even succeed in making him or her ill—something he or she won't soon forget. Keep in mind, too, that *your* opinion of what might be daring or ethnic, might not be the same thing that your client would consider edgy. Even a cozy Italian restaurant might be considered to be an ethnic restaurant by some people.

I have offered to turn my guests on to sushi if they have never had it before, and sometimes they are willing to give it a shot (although I will always order a cooked dish, too, just in case the sushi doesn't suit them). It's always better to have too much food rather than not enough. If we ordered too much food, I suggest they take the remainder back to his or her office. They can either look to be a hero by sharing the leftovers with the support staff, or enjoy it at home later. Either way, it contributes to making lunch more fun, and makes your client feel good about his or her relationship with you.

I have learned which of my clients are open to trying something exotic, such as Vietnamese cuisine, and which ones would never stray from good, old-fashioned comfort food such as meatloaf and mashed potatoes. For example, I have a client who would never eat at an Indian restaurant. And she has no problem with Chinese food, but she believes she wouldn't enjoy Japanese. If you are ever out to lunch and are asked to do the ordering for the entire table, make sure you have enough variety, as well as enough food.

I have a friend and former client, Robyn, who currently works as a freelance writer. She told me a story recently about a lunch date she had when she was a college intern. She had a meeting with the executive director of a state government agency. He ordered moo shu shrimp for their lunch. Robyn doesn't eat shrimp, but being young and inexperienced, she didn't know how to tell him that she didn't want that for lunch. Unfortunately, that was *all* he ordered! She had no alternative. She said she managed to "choke it down with about three Cokes!"

Had Robyn been this man's client, he would have lost big points. They have remained friends. She told me that she confessed to him two years later. He was upset and asked her why she hadn't told him she didn't like shrimp when he was ordering.

As a young student, Robyn didn't know how to express herself, or her preferences, at the time. This has to make you wonder if a client would tell you if you were ordering something he or she didn't care for. Be sure to ask your guests what they prefer. And if you are going to insist that they try something that you love, make sure that you order a few other dishes in case your favorite isn't to their liking.

What to avoid

When ordering, keep in mind that some foods are also easier to eat than others. Spaghetti and meatballs can end up everywhere (aside from the fact that slurping noodles does not make way for good contract negotiations!). I believe that noodles are the one entrée that you should *never* order at a business lunch—especially when served in a red sauce! I had lunch with an attorney recently who said he didn't order noodles, because the last thing his wife said to him when he left the house that morning was, "Try not to spill anything on yourself!" Good advice, especially if you have trouble finding your mouth, as we all do occasionally.

Avoid ordering any foods that may be considered "challenging" to eat, such as barbequed ribs, or *anything* with red sauce! Corn on the cob is an obvious no-no. You can also end up wearing your lunch if you crack into a lobster or crab legs. Chocolate fondue is another menu item you might want to save for eating with friends. Picture yourself with a stain on your shirt when presenting a six-figure contract to your client! Would *you* sign that deal with confidence in your host? Order food that is manageable whenever possible, and always take small bites.

Timing is everything

Choose your time carefully, too. Most restaurants have a rush at noon. Service is slower, and tables are scarce. The rooms get crowded and noisy. If you have a very important luncheon booked, and you need to talk about numbers or review a proposal, do yourself a favor and avoid the noon rush. See if your client can meet you at 11:30 a.m., and get to the business at hand right away. Or you can meet at 1 p.m., and you'll have a nice, quiet, peaceful lunch—and be able to discuss everything that you had on your agenda as the restaurant empties out.

Not only is the time of day important, so is the day of the week. Mondays and Tuesdays seem to play host to many internal meetings. On Fridays, business can become a little sloppy. Aside from being casual Friday in many offices, it has also become a half-day for some businesses. If you have a very important meeting, try to make it earlier in the week. I believe you should have a business lunch or breakfast at least five times a week, but they won't all be intense meetings. Schedule your longtime clients for a Friday afternoon. They may not have to go back to work, and you can both relax and share some quality time.

Alternative lunches

Do you have a client who loves racing? You could take him or her to a racetrack—if there is one where you live—for a really exciting break in the day. You could even take him or her to a miniature grand-prix-style racetrack, for a special business lunch. Driving a miniature racecar would certainly clear the cobwebs from what would otherwise be a typical day at the office.

We even have a restaurant in Las Vegas that offers mini-bowling. If you know of a place such as that, you and a client could play a couple of games while waiting for your lunch to be served, and return to work feeling as though you had a small vacation! I always figure that an hour is an hour, and you can spend it creating a memorable event just as easily as you can go grab a burger or a salad.

Use your judgment, though. You probably wouldn't want to get too creative with a brand new client. You will benefit more by learning what each client's likes and dislikes are before delivering a creative surprise. I had a client who always wanted a red Porsche. Costco happened to be selling toy cars for about $15, and they had exactly the car he wanted—just a whole lot smaller. I delivered it to him with a card that read, "Just what you've always wanted!" He loved the gift, and from that point on, he always called me his favorite rep—the one who could deliver whatever he wanted. I know how much he appreciated the gesture, as I heard about it from other salespeople who called on him.

More than 10 years ago, Cleveland cleaned up its downtown area and succeeded in creating a hot spot down on the Cuyahoga River. Most of the restaurants and clubs at "The Flats" had "riverside" parking—so you could dock your boat at the restaurant, enjoy your lunch or dinner, and continue on with your boat ride. Imagine meeting your client at one of these riverside restaurants, and taking him or her for a cruise up the river for your "business" lunch. That would be refreshing, and so much fun! If you didn't own a boat, you could rent one. Perhaps someone in your networking circle has one, and you could instigate a great outing with him or her.

I'm sure that wherever you live there are exciting opportunities to make an impact and impress your clients, either through creative modes of transportation, or through variations on a typical business lunch.

We have an annual event in Las Vegas called "The Street of Dreams" that showcases million-dollar homes with every feature imaginable. I was able to take a tough client "out to lunch" by suggesting we visit "The Street of Dreams" instead of going out for a traditional lunch. She absolutely loved the idea and jumped at the chance (she was a restaurant owner for whom the thought of "just going to lunch" wasn't very appealing).

Once you know what a client would enjoy, you can deliver his or her "dream" to them and create a sensation! Again, you are only limited by your creativity.

Chapter 6

The Secret to Cell Phone Etiquette

*Always remember to
turn your cell phone
OFF!*

W hat's that? Oh my goodness! You're in the middle of discussing your client's budget for the coming year and your cell phone is ringing! Unless you have a family member in the hospital, remember to turn your phone off when you meet your client. If you have forgotten to turn it off (I'm pretty sure we all have at times), it is best to apologize, decline to accept the call with the push of a button, and then turn it off immediately. Another apology doesn't hurt. Your immediate response will be appreciated.

Cell phone usage is *not* a two-way street!

But what if your *clients'* phone rings during lunch, dinner, or your presentation? Unfortunately, it's not a two-way street. They are your client. And if they want to, they can leave you sitting there for 20 minutes or more while they chat on their cell phone! You are there to cater to *them* and to make *them* feel comfortable, so if they choose to take a call they have received while you're together, then you have no choice but to let them.

You can excuse yourself and go to the restroom, which is a nice gesture, as it affords them some privacy for their call should they need it. You can open up your proposal or day planner and make some notes, or take out your PDA and do some work. For the most part, you can assume that the call is necessary, or they would offer to return the call when they are done with lunch.

For some, however, staying on the call may be a power play. They are the clients and they know it. Whatever their motive, they can do what they want. I always feel that whenever a call interrupts your meeting, your nice clients genuinely feel apologetic for having to take the call. The good news is that this can usually work to your favor, as you will have their undivided attention once they hang up.

What can you do if you have a critical situation pending, such as a loved one in the hospital, your dog at the veterinarian's, or you are waiting for lab results? Many times we have our own, urgent circumstances. If that's the case, and you are not on a crucial first meeting with a new client, I believe you should tell your client as soon as you are seated that you are waiting for a call from the doctor, hospital, or clinic, and ask if he or she would mind terribly if you took the call when it comes in. Promise to be as *brief* as possible, and then follow through by keeping the call short. There are so few things that can't wait an hour—other than medical emergencies.

On the other hand, if you *are* with a new, first-time client, you might want to try calling whoever is at the heart of the emergency situation *before* you rendezvous with your client, or immediately after leaving him or her. Again, there are very few circumstances in which an hour is going to make a huge difference.

Cell phones are here to stay, and they are for *our* convenience! However, when you become a slave to yours, you risk being rude to your guests.

Chapter 7

The Flow: Being Prepared to Assure Smooth Sailing

Be prepared and informed
so you can carry on a
casual, topical conversation.

Once you accept that sharing a meal with someone is an important step in building your relationships, why would you not have breakfast, lunch, or dinner meetings scheduled five, eight, or 10 times a week? Knowing the value of something and not applying it is a tragic mistake. But for many people, business lunches can be as awkward as a blind date: uncomfortable silence, bad service, not knowing what to talk about. We've all been there.

If you can't handle this kind of social activity, there are two things you can do. First, you can learn to handle it so well that you actually begin to *enjoy* doing business this way. Or, second, you could consider changing careers.

Being reluctant to meet your clients socially, when you are in a relationship-based business, is always going to hold you back professionally. Your competition will get more of your business (and may even kill your business).

One of the best ways to begin to enjoy business lunches, meals, or mixers is by being prepared. If you are really uncomfortable with the thought of dining with strangers, try role playing at home. You can practice with your family or friends. I used to hate role-playing, but I have learned that it really helps you over those hurdles that spring up along the way. There is nothing as comforting as being prepared for anything that might come up. Though we can't predict every possible situation, we can certainly plan for the basics.

Have some idea of what you are going to discuss. You will know going in what you want to accomplish. Are you just going to get to know your client? Do you actually need to tell him or her about your product, and services, or details about your business? Are you going to present him or her with a proposal?

Let's look at getting to know your client. Be prepared to ask questions, but be careful—don't assume too much familiarity too soon. Learn to judge what's acceptable with each new client. Don't fire off questions as though you're leading a Senate investigative hearing! Listen to what he or she tells you and respond with interest. Don't hurry to ask the next question without acknowledging or exploring the answer to the last question. Listen carefully to their answers and find a way to relate to them.

We've all been out with people with whom we have little in common. For instance, what if you are out with a client whose home life is nothing like yours? Maybe you come from a large family, and your client was an only child. Maybe he or she is married and has children, and you are single. It may be challenging to find the common ground, but it's out there. For example, if your client is a parent and tells you he or she is dealing with a problem at home (perhaps his or her teenager is having trouble at school), you don't have to be a parent to sympathize. Remember that questions pull and statements push.

Ask questions. Why is his or her child having trouble at school? What kind of trouble is he or she having? Maybe he or she is hanging out with the wrong kids. Maybe he or she is having difficulty with scholastics. A sympathetic ear will get you a lot farther than anything else at that point.

You can always ask, "What are you going to do about it?," or "Are you getting any help, either from the school or a counselor?" I have even given out a psychologist's number, or recommended a helpful book to some clients. Even if my client doesn't ever read it, he or she will know that I was concerned and was doing my best to help him or her. And if you don't have kids yourself, know how much caring is reflected by offering a compassionate, "I can imagine what you must be going through." Ask questions and you'll be surprised what you will learn!

After your lunch, make notes on any subjects you covered, and follow up the next time you see or speak with your client. If you ask how his or her son has been doing in school lately, he or she will know you were listening and will appreciate finding out how much you sincerely care about him or her, and his or her well-being.

Dollars and sense

Be aware of your client's financial position. You probably don't know his or her exact bottom line (nor should you), but if someone seems to have a modest lifestyle, don't go on about your recent trip to Australia, the new jewelry you bought for your wife, or your new car! People get jealous, and you don't need those emotions interfering in your relationship.

I have a friend who was a salesperson in the same industry in which I worked. She is very well-off. We have both called on a lot of the same clients. Many of them have told me how tired they were of hearing about this woman's lifestyle. She is a successful, wonderful, fun salesperson—but she forgets that not everyone is doing as well as she is! My clients have called me and asked if I could join them for lunch with her, so they "wouldn't have to spend the entire lunch hearing about her latest trip to Europe, or about her new house." Always be thoughtful and aware of your client's position and situation.

In advertising we accepted a lot in trade (tickets for shows, scrip for restaurants, and so on). Even our well-heeled clients loved to get free tickets, especially when they have company visiting. I always felt like Santa Clause when we had a windfall of goodies that we could offer our clients. The clients who were struggling financially were so appreciative of getting a dinner at a gourmet restaurant, or a free night out on the town, that it became a perk of my job to be able to share our trade.

Be prepared for casual conversation

Make it a point to know at least a little bit about a lot. Be prepared for casual conversation. I am always teasing one friend because he *invents* things—that already exist. I tell him that he needs to spend more time out and about (he works a lot of hours, so his exposure to new trends and people is limited). This happens to a lot of us who are overloaded and overwhelmed, and we may feel as though we are out of touch with the rest of the world. That just won't do in business.

Being prepared for casual conversation is one of the best ways to assure that your business lunch will flow smoothly. One way to prepare is to become knowledge-able about a vast array of subjects, such as current events, trends, the entertainment industry, and your community. Always watch at least a portion of a national morning news show, especially on a day when you have a business lunch. Even just a few minutes of viewing or listening while you get ready for work will get you up to date on the day's news and current events. I also recommend watching a variety of shows, including entertainment news.

Talking about ideas is the sign of a great person, and wonderful things can come from sharing ideas. But if your business relationship is new and you are looking for innocent subjects to discuss, it's always great fun to be in-the-know about celebrities, actors, singers, and public figures. These are all subjects and topics that will prepare you for making great conversation during lunch. You will want to avoid **all** controversial topics, which I cover in depth in Chapter 10.

You will be able to participate intelligently in almost any conversation when you are in touch with what is going on in the world around you. Read a wide assortment of magazines, too. *Newsweek* and *Time* will give you newsworthy subjects to discuss over lunch, and the latest issue of *People* magazine will always have some interesting stories to share. I began subscribing to *Entrepreneur* and I love it—the magazine features the latest cutting-edge technology, discoveries, and business (which gives me a lot to talk about!). If you read *Living*, or other lifestyle, living, or cooking magazines, you can round out your knowledge of topical material. Of course, if your client introduces a subject, try to stick with that, or something that is related to it. If you don't know much about their chosen topic, ask them questions about it.

You should strive to have a basic knowledge or understanding about almost everything, even when it comes to something that might not ordinarily interest you. I like to play golf, but I don't have the time for team sports. That doesn't mean I can't have a conversation about them. "Who do you like in this weekend's football game?" If your client is a football fan, that's all he or she would need to hear to get excited about the game. You can ask why he or she prefers his or her favorite team. If my client feels that he or she is an expert on the subject—because he or she knows so much more about the sport or team than I do—then I have succeeded in making him or her feel good, which is my main goal in the first place!

Try to find common ground. Sometimes a simple reference will take you into 20 minutes of great conversation. I might mention that I worked in my garden the past weekend, and my client and I could be off and running, talking about which plants do best in the desert soil and which nursery has the best selection.

Insider tips on any subject are always appreciated. If you know something special about a subject that you and your client have found in common, share your inside information with him or her—where to find the best sugar-free, homemade chocolates, who's the best veterinarian in the area, and so on. Any of these helpful hints will not only provide you with a reason to call your client to follow up, but they will also work to bond the two of you by your common interest.

Some people love to talk about fashion. I remember calling on a new client (who is now a friend) when he was a marketing director in the casino industry. He told me about the suits he used to get at a discount store when he was just out of college, and how the pinstripes on the discount suits never quite matched up. I always make certain to comment on how sharp and fashionable his suits are now, 15 years later. He is currently a vice president, and I knew him when—and that in itself is always great common ground

If you are unfamiliar with the subject that your client wants to discuss (and you've already asked questions about it, and made him or her feel great), and you want to change the subject, you can do so by *bumping* the conversation a bit. If your client is talking about a subject that makes you uneasy, or that you find unfamiliar, here is a simple example of a way to change it—without noticeably changing it.

In Las Vegas, Nevada, we have very few natives (everyone is from somewhere else!). If I was having lunch with a client who sat down and started talking about Sunday's game, and how much he or she likes the Green Bay Packers, I would likely ask if he or she were originally from Wisconsin. If they said yes, I might ask what life was like in Wisconsin, and how he or she came to live here. Without getting into a big discussion about football, we are now talking about the client's hometown, what makes it special, and so on.

If he or she is not from Wisconsin, then I would ask why the Packers are his or her favorite team. Then I might ask where he or she is from originally, searching for that all-important common ground. He or she is going to come away thinking I know a lot about football, Las Vegas, maybe even something about his or her hometown. He or she will also know that I not only care about him or her, but that I am interested in the choices he or she has made. Learn a little about a lot, and your conversations will flow with ease.

I once met an American salesman who lived and worked in Japan. When we talked about his specific challenges, he said he hadn't realized how important it was to be prepared—even just for casual conversation! He admitted that he had been to lunches where he and his clients actually discussed the weather and the humidity, and said those lunches were incredibly awkward. He also has dealt with cultural challenges. If you are working in a country that is culturally different from your own, make sure that you are aware of all of the differences, so that you do not unwittingly offend your clients. Check with local resources or associates to educate yourself on what is acceptable behavior—from conversational topics to manners—and then respect those guidelines. You can even pick up a book on foreign etiquette. Again, be prepared. A little homework will really pay off for you with great dividends.

When to bring up the subject of business

Now, let's talk about actually trying to sell something, and how to make a presentation during a business lunch. Remember: Timing is everything, and how things are flowing is extremely important in deciding when to bring up the subject of business. If you have just been seated, and the conversation is flowing smoothly, don't interrupt by whipping out a proposal just yet. Enjoy the conversation. If you listen intently, you will almost always learn something that will help you with your presentation.

Sometimes, I will offer the choice to my client as to when they would like to discuss a proposal. I might say, "Would you like to see what I brought for you now? Or would you

rather enjoy our lunch first?" If they are on a tight schedule, they may appreciate being able to get right to the business portion of the lunch. It is also helpful to make such a
suggestion with enthusiasm, if what you have brought him
or her is exciting or compelling. Imagine if you were the
client and you sat down to lunch and your account manager said, "I'm *so* glad you're here. I couldn't *wait* to show
you what I am working on for you! Let me go over this
with you right away, so we can discuss it over lunch!" How
anxious and excited would you be to see what he or she
has for you? You would likely be filled with anticipation,
and that would put you in a great, receptive mood!

As the host or hostess, make sure you order your beverages, and perhaps an appetizer, and then dive in to your
proposal with sustained enthusiasm. You'll be surprised
at how contagious your enthusiasm will be.

If, on the contrary, you can put off your presentation
until after you've eaten, you can turn the lunch itself into
a great, fact-finding mission. Unless you feel certain that
your client is anxious to see what you have brought him
or her, and he or she is as excited as you are about getting a look at it, you will find that waiting until after lunch
is a better option. But don't wait too long after lunch has
been served and cleared, or you may find your presentation could be cut short. (It's always a good thing to inquire about your client's schedule. It never hurts to ask
if he or she is in a hurry, or if he or she has time to spare.)
Most people will give you some kind of time frame. By
establishing this up front, you will know when to turn the
subject to business.

Then, during lunch, ask the right questions and listen carefully to the answers, so you will be better armed for your presentation when the time comes. Once the dishes have been cleared and you've ordered a round of coffee or dessert for the table, you'll be able to delve into the business at hand.

However, if your main goal is to establish a relationship (and you haven't planned a formal presentation), then let your client decide when to bring up the subject of business, *if at all.*

If you are going to wait until after your meal to present, then during your meal be sure to ask questions about your client's business and any changes that they may be experiencing. If it is appropriate, and your client seems comfortable, you can ask questions about his or her home life. Stick to the basics—innocent subjects such as whether or not he or she is married, or if he or she has kids or pets.

Ask open-ended questions that will encourage good conversation. For example, what does he or she feel are his or her greatest challenges? And what does the future hold for his or her company? Find out facts that will help you when you present to him or her. A successful fact-finding mission may also help you to overcome objections as they come up during your presentation.

Everyone has an opinion, and most people are anxious to share theirs! Don't forget to ask questions! It's the best way to learn about business, competition, the city where you live, even what's going on in our country. What is happening in those realms, and your client's opinion on them, is a great way to build a conversation. Remember the client's answers, and write down anything significant as soon as you are alone (so that you can reference your notes later).

When you have finished your meal and the dishes have been cleared, it's time to get down to business. What I said about presenting your proposal with enthusiasm applies to presenting *after* lunch, as well. Use all of the information you have just acquired to show how your product or service relates to your client's business and how you can become part of the solution for his or her company's challenges.

Here is a great example of putting newly gained knowledge to work during a presentation. Imagine that during the course of a luncheon, your client told you that his or her company had just experienced layoffs. You had hoped to sell him or her a new computer system. It's easy enough for a client to object to any new expenditure, especially if it is for a product or a service that he or she already has. But when faced with dramatic budget cuts or layoffs, as so many companies are, it is easy for him or her to say no to any new costs. But because you asked the right questions, and listened during lunch, you would know that your client's company is cutting back. Now you could put a new spin on your proposal. Perhaps your new computer system can do the work of three people! Maybe its applications will actually take care of some of the workload created by the new vacancies.

If you were presenting cold, to someone you hardly knew, and didn't have the opportunity to gain some insight into his or her company, you might be caught off guard when he or she told you in the middle of your presentation that things are so tight that he or she has had cutbacks or layoffs.

But because you took this client to lunch, asked questions, listened, and learned what his or her company was experiencing, you now have an advantage. You can present your new product; touch on the highlights, features, and benefits, just as you had planned. Then, you can confidently disclose that, although your product would have been an excellent option before—it is now even *more* perfect for your client, *especially* in light of the budget crunch or diminished staff. How could they afford *not* to upgrade? Now, you and your product or services have become part of the solution. And, because you had time to think about how you could really help him or her, you have not only turned the situation around, but you have closed your deal.

Tell the truth

Back when laptop computers first came out, I had a first lunch date with a prospect, Amy, who was the director of advertising and marketing at a downtown casino/hotel. Amy was anxious to get to the materials I had brought. I was able to pull up our latest research in bright, colorful charts—right at the table! Without a laptop, I could have shown my client the very same charts printed out exactly as they were on the computer, but on "boring" paper instead. There was something about the new technology that made my presentation so dynamic, so exciting, and so different. Add to that the fact that the numbers I was presenting to her corroborated her own research with regard to who her customer base was—what casino games they preferred to play, how long they stayed, where they came from, and so on—and she was sold.

She knew that I was telling her the truth. But the fact that I was telling it to her in such a new, exciting format got her so excited that she wanted to start advertising with me immediately. It was all about timing, flow, and selling with excitement.

In that instance, we had gone over everything by the time our lunch was served. We visited through the remainder of the lunch, referring back to the information I had covered in my presentation. We even made a golf date for the weekend! The best part was that I was selling her something she really needed for her casino. Had I not convinced her to buy with me, I would have done her a disservice.

Keep in mind that no matter how friendly you may become with your clients, or how comfortable you become at taking them to lunch, you still need to be at the top of your game competitively. You need to be prepared and informed. You need to know as much as possible about your client, and his or her business—as well as his or her competition, your competition, and your industry. All the schmoozing in the world won't make up for incompetence!

Sometimes, you will present information that your client will need to take back to his or her office to share with other decision-makers. Although you should always try to build your relationships with the key decision-makers, not all businesses lend themselves to a single voice. In advertising, we often had to deal with advertising agencies who then would present to their clients. In that case, be patient, and suggest that they call you with any questions.

It is helpful to have deadlines, or special offers, to ensure quicker decisions. Roger Dawson is one of the country's best-known experts at the art of negotiating. In his book *Secrets of Power Negotiating* (Career Press, 2000), he identifies time as a key factor (or "pressure point") in any negotiation. Whenever you can incorporate an incentive for a quick decision into your proposal, you will see faster results.

Keep in mind, though, that if you plan on doing business with this client for years to come, a few days or weeks is not *too long to wait*, especially for a big decision or sale. People can tell when they are being hustled and do not respond well to pushy or forceful tactics. I have always tried to be on my clients' side, searching for ways to help them to do their business successfully. It shows, too, in the loyalty of my clients and in the long-standing relationships that I have formed.

After lunch, finalize the details of your next contact. Ask to call the following day, or ask the client when he or she expect to have an answer to your proposal. Also let him or her know you will send any necessary additional information as soon as you get back to your office. Take advantage of whatever has transpired at lunch to generate an opening for your follow-up call.

Be aware of his or her time, as well. If he or she has glanced more than once at his or her watch, let the client get back to work. He or she doesn't need to hang around while you settle the check (if you haven't already taken care of it). Tell your client that you know he or she has to get back to the office and that you will finish up at the restaurant.

If you picked him or her up and drove to the luncheon, make sure you don't make him or her late in getting back to the office. Always take care of the check as discreetly as possible. And always tip generously. Being cheap is an undesirable quality, and who wants to do business with someone who doesn't take good care of those who are helpful to them? (In Chapter 12, I will teach you several ways to settle the check discreetly and creatively.)

Chapter 8

Fair-Weather Friends

Change a life: Take an
unemployed former client
to a networking luncheon.

I have formed a number of lasting relationships by taking care of clients when they were unemployed. Anyone can be a fair-weather friend, but if an account executive takes you out to lunch when you are unemployed, you don't have a budget, and he or she has little or nothing to gain by socializing with you, you would likely remember that person when you are back on top. You would realize that he or she is being kind. And think about it—no client is ever out of the picture completely.

Clients have feelings, too

One of my clients/friends used to be a marketing director at a major resort on the Las Vegas strip. She had a multi-million-dollar budget and a *lot* of "friends." She changed jobs and went to work in the public relations department of a large advertising agency. That meant that she was no longer in charge of buying advertising for a major property. She no longer had a budget to spread around. She was appalled at what happened.

She found that the account managers who had been so friendly to her at her previous job would not even return her phone calls now! She had a rude awakening when she realized that it was her budget, not her companionship or friendship, that they had wanted.

Most everyone wants to be popular or well-liked, and it's a bitter pill to swallow if you learn that it was your money or your position that people liked most about you.

Never be the kind of person who breaks someone's heart or spirit. Clients have feelings, too! Always be there for the people in your life. If you took someone to lunch when he or she was doing well, remember to take him or her to lunch when he or she is down. It will make him or her feel special and important.

As an added benefit, you will find that taking care of people—whether or not they are in a position to help you—will make you feel good about yourself, too. If you can ever help someone find a new job, you will win the fierce loyalty of that person for the rest of your life. People know that you are working, and that you are a part of their lives because of business. But if they discover that you are there even when the chips are down, or "just because," they will appreciate you more than ever.

A simple way to change someone's life

Always stay in touch with your former clients. If you can't take the time to meet them for lunch or breakfast, drop them a note or a quick e-mail, or pick up the phone. Networking and cultivating relationships is always a worthwhile way to spend time. And remember: A little caring goes a long way with someone who is unemployed!

One of the best things you can do for a former client who is currently unemployed is to take them to a networking luncheon or event. Many of us belong to more than one professional networking organization, and these organizations will often host a monthly luncheon, break-fast, or mixer. If your unemployed former client can make a connection with someone that will eventually lead him or her to a new job or career, he or she will have you to thank. Even if nothing comes of the event, he or she will come away knowing that you were looking out for him or her. This is a gesture that can literally change someone's life!

Imagine if a connection he or she made at the event to which you took them turns into a solid job opportunity! This is similar to the vast difference illustrated by the old saying, "Give a man a fish and he'll eat for a day; *teach* a man to fish and he will eat for the rest of his life." When you take someone to lunch, he or she will eat that day. But if you help him or her to find a job, he or she may be able to eat for the rest of his or her life—all because of an introduction that came about when *you* provided the opportunity. Imagine the ripple effect that you can create simply by taking someone to lunch!

I was the job bank director for Las Vegas Women in Communications (WIC) for three years. It was one of the most satisfying positions I've ever held. I really had a knack for matching qualified candidates to the right jobs. But it didn't stop there. Some 15 years later, people *still* forward resumes and job opportunities to me because they know that if I'm aware of anyone who is looking, I will pass along the information discreetly.

One time I found a job for the wife of one of my boss's friends. She and her husband had just moved here from New York, where she worked in the fashion industry. She didn't know what she was qualified to do, because she couldn't do the same work that she had done in New York.

I helped her to find a job selling advertising for a visitor publication. The timing was great, and she clicked with the publisher. It turned out that, in a short time, she was making more money than *most* of us! She remained at the job four years. When she finally parted ways with that publisher, she immediately secured a job with another magazine. A mutual friend of ours said, "She went from having the *best* job in town to having the *new, best* job in town!"

Her new job lasted several more years, and now, I'm happy to say, she's retired! And she earned it. With just one phone call, her life was significantly changed—along with all of the other lives that her work and influence has touched. That was truly the ripple effect in action—drop a pebble into a pond, and the ripples never end. Find someone a job, and the ripples will never end, either.

Never be a fair-weather friend. Don't cut people out of your life just because they are no longer in a position to help you.

Chapter 9

Do's and Don'ts

Follow the leader
when it comes to
alcohol or dessert.

Certain behaviors can be easily misinterpreted, especially in business situations. There are several touchy situations, from issues arising from gender differences, to getting drunk in front of your clients. There are also several behaviors you can adopt in order to make your clients feel comfortable and accepted.

Drinking

Let's talk about alcohol consumption for starters. In *social* situations, one usually never wants to get sloppy in front of friends. But in *business* settings, getting drunk is a ticket to disaster! Even getting a little "buzzed" can be a dangerous thing to do, too, especially when you are dealing with business associates.

It may *seem* harmless enough to have a few drinks when you are out with clients, but remember that alcohol can make you sloppy, slurry, and stupid. If everyone is having a few drinks, you may never notice! But if you are the only one in a group who is *not* drinking, then you know that the drinkers think they are doing fine when it's obvious they are not. You never know when you might slip and say the wrong thing to the wrong person.

So, generally speaking—when in doubt, don't! That being said, I really don't think there is anything wrong with having an occasional drink with a client, or at a mixer. I do, however, advocate moderation and discretion.

Wait a little longer…we'll get a much better deal after Gibson's had his third martini!

What's the *worst* that could happen?

A few years ago, I was involved in the following scenario. (And if I may borrow a line from the old TV show, *The FBI*, "The events you are about to witness are true. Only the names have been changed to protect the innocent.")

The company I worked for took some preferred clients on a trip from Las Vegas to San Diego to see a Padres baseball game. Though it sure beat a day at the office, one of my coworkers forgot that it was still work. Being a white-knuckle flyer, I met this coworker (whom I'll refer to as Patty) in the airport bar shortly before our departure. I had one cocktail and she had two.

The flight to San Diego takes about an hour. While in the air, Patty consumed *five* vodkas—on the rocks! I had cautioned her to take it easy, but she was on a mission to have fun. I realized that, although Patty was quite drunk by the time the plane landed, she wasn't nearly as drunk as she was *going* to be.

As we were getting off the plane, Patty smacked the man in front of her on his shoulder and said loudly, "Who are you? You must be pretty important if you're on this plane with *us!* Because we only brought our *biggest* clients!" I took her arm and told her whom she had just hit, but Patty really didn't think she'd done anything wrong. She thought the man would be flattered to hear he was a big client (as if he didn't already know!)

Outside the airport, waiting for our shuttle, Patty was a "party" of one. She was whooping and hollering, and having a great time. She kept announcing "We're in Sa-a-a-n Diego!"

My boss asked one of our associates, Beth, to tell Patty to settle down. Without a thought other than to please the boss, Beth walked over to Patty and told her politely to settle down. Patty was belligerent, as most drunks are, and told Beth to "lighten up!"

Beth moved a little closer to Patty and told her that *our boss* wanted her to settle down, in the hopes that if she learned where the directive had originated she might be more receptive.

As Beth walked away, Patty shouted, "Do you know what your problem is?" (By that time, everyone in our group was looking at them.) Beth looked back at Patty, but didn't say a word. Patty then hollered, "Your problem is that you're a Jew!"

The silence after Patty's remark, as we all stood breathless, was deafening. Everyone had heard her loud and clear. Her next declaration further illustrated just how drunk she was. "Now if you was from Texas," Patty shouted, "you'd *know* how to party!" Our clients and associates, many of whom were Jewish, were understandably appalled. Do you think those clients would *ever* work with Patty again, or even a company that tolerated this behavior? I was surprised she wasn't terminated on the spot.

Later, after she had slept it off, I asked her if she remembered what she had said. She did not, of course, nor was she interested in learning about it. I had to share a room with her that weekend, but that was the end of our friendship. She also managed to alienate about 10 of our clients—clients who were on the trip with us because, as Patty had drunkenly pointed out, they were our *biggest* clients! That's a sobering story for anyone who drinks.

As I said, getting a little buzzed in front of your friends is usually okay, as long as you are not driving. But if you think that you can handle getting drunk in front of your clients, think again!

Follow the leader

At a business lunch, it's "follow the leader." The popular technique of "mirroring" your clients is the best rule; in other words, do what they do. If your client wants to have a cocktail, there should be no harm in having one. And the lighter, the better. If your client orders a glass of wine, you might want to order a wine spritzer, which is made with just a little bit of wine mixed with soda. I used to have a client who got drunk easily, even after consuming just one glass of wine. A spritzer was her answer to being able to drink while out with her own clients. It helped her to feel that she was joining in. The only problem was that she would feel so good from the spritzer, she'd switch to wine—and then it was only a matter of time before she'd be quite drunk. In addition, she was often on a diet, so most of the time she was drinking on an empty stomach, which didn't help matters at all. She got a reputation as a big drinker. I knew she never had more than one or two glasses of wine, but what she did drink would hit her so hard that folks thought she must be drinking quite heavily. That's a reputation we could all do without!

It's best for business if you can go along with your clients or your boss in some way. In fact, a television ad for Samuel Adams beer showed a boss with three employees ordering drinks at lunch: Each of the three employees ordered non-alcoholic drinks in front of the boss—water and iced tea—until the boss ordered a beer. Then they all tried to make light of the situation by changing their orders to Sam Adams. This commercial made the employees look ridiculous. But we can learn from this advertisement. Ask your client (or boss) what he or she would like to drink *before* you order.

Having a drink with a client doesn't always have to be a drama or a disaster. I had taken a client to lunch on a hot fall day, and she wanted to know if it was okay to order a glass of wine. Tanya had just finished working on her budgets, sold her home, and closed on a new one the night before. She just wanted to unwind. I told her that she could have whatever she wanted. She said she felt funny having a drink in the middle of the day, but, nonetheless, she wanted one.

We each had one glass of wine and a lovely lunch, sitting outside at Cili, overlooking the Bali Hai Golf Course. It was a beautiful fall day. No harm done. In fact, it was so relaxing that it felt as if we were out on a Saturday. We finished our lunch with some café lattes, and then we both went back to work. We had a wonderful time. She sent me a great thank-you note—and said that she had been working so hard on budgets, that the lunch had been the highlight of her week. Moments like that really help to build relationships. Coincidentally, a month or so later, when her budget was cut and she had to cancel some advertising, she cut everyone but me.

Be your own person

Knowing that it is best for business to go along with your clients is a great reason to frequent the same restaurant, especially if you are *not* a drinker. You can let your hostess, waiter, or bartender know that if you ever order your "usual," that they should bring you a club soda with a twist. Sometimes, it's best to just play along and not make a big deal out of something! No job should ever make you feel that you should have to consume alcohol. But the bottom line here is that you ultimately want to make your client feel comfortable. Mirroring his or her behavior makes him or her feel accepted. By ordering your "'usual," you appear to be drinking along with him or her, and he or she is having fun—not feeling like he or she is doing anything wrong.

Still, some people still insist that if they are having a drink, you should join them. If you are not at one of your "regular" restaurants, there's a way to handle this if you don't want to have a drink. You can excuse yourself and go to the restroom. On the way there, find your waiter and give him your "usual" order discreetly. Another way to handle it is to order a spritzer or other light drink, and then just don't drink it. The odds are your client will never notice. If he or she does, you can just say it doesn't taste good to you. Meanwhile, he or she has a drink and is happy, and is not feeling as though you are sitting in judgment against him or her.

An agent with Coldwell Banker Realty, Nancy Kurtik, recalled a time many years ago when she worked in the marketing department for a major airline. She remembered that a rep from her advertising agency loved to take her and her associates to a Mexican restaurant in Hermosa Beach, where they would be shown the new campaign ideas and then order margaritas. "It never failed that lunch bled into dinner and dinner into cabs. It was all a big waste

133

of time," she said. "And it didn't do anything to help my marriage, either! The agency got sold and the airline was taken over by a conservative group out of Texas!" So in the end, what was accomplished? It sounds as though the agency people were just using business as an excuse to get drunk!

You may have been out to lunch with friends when it's someone's birthday or there is a special occasion to celebrate. Little thought goes into buying a round of drinks for the table and drinking a toast to something special—basically pretending it's happy hour in the middle of the day. The smart ones who do this on occasion will make sure that they eat a nice lunch, and perhaps have a cup of coffee, before returning to the office. It's not the end of the world to have a drink at lunchtime for most people.

If, for any reason, you are uncomfortable with having a drink at a business lunch, there are a lot of excuses for not drinking that won't be perceived as judgmental by your clients. You can always tell a "little white lie" and say that you are taking medication that can't be mixed with alcohol, or that you just aren't feeling 100 percent that day. I am not advocating outright lying or misrepresentation. Instead, think of it as how you would answer a friend if he or she asked you, "Do these pants make my butt look big?" This may sound underhanded, but remember that you are trying to make your clients feel comfortable. If you feel it's wrong to consume alcohol at a business lunch, you could discreetly decline. However, you may run the risk of making your client feel uneasy about having a drink. As I said, no boss should ever make you feel that drinking is a part of your job (unless you are a wine salesman!).

Avoiding the "battle of the sexes"

Erv Nelson, of Nelson & Associates, is an attorney. One of the best pieces of advice I have ever heard is contained in "Erv's Rule:" *Never have business lunches with just one person of the opposite sex.*

Nelson knows about things such as this, and how they can get you in trouble. It may take some extra effort or planning on your part, but by always having a third party at business lunches, you will protect yourself and your company from any unjust lawsuits, rumors, and even plain old gossip. Imagine you are a happily married man having a fun, but strictly business lunch, with a female associate. A friend of your wife's sees you there, obviously enjoying yourself, with an attractive woman. *You* know that you are working with your client, rep, or coworker. But to an outsider, it may look suspicious. So, your wife's friend can't wait to telephone your wife to "inquire" as to your whereabouts. It is a waste of time in my opinion—but there are people out there who live for this sort of gossip opportunity. Why give them ammunition?

If you know you are going to meet someone of the opposite sex, whether for a first-time business lunch, a casual business lunch, or a job interview, take along an associate—of the same sex as your guest—if possible. I realize that this can interfere with the feeling of intimacy created by sharing quality one-on-one time together. Sometimes, however, it is better to be on the safe side and sacrifice that intimacy for a more professional environment, especially for a *first* meeting.

One of the best solutions is to bring along a third party who would enjoy meeting your client or associate. You can actually accomplish a small bit of networking by introducing them to each other. Introducing clients and associates to each other can work well, as they will each benefit from the relationship and remember that it was *you* who originally brought them together.

The good old days of power lunching are history!

The times are certainly changing and the old three-martini power lunches are hopefully a thing of the past. I came across an outdated guide to power lunching, and I get the biggest kick out of reading a passage or two to my audiences whenever I'm speaking at a seminar. I offer a prize to anyone who can identify the year in which it was written. So far, I've only had to give out one prize. See if you can figure it out. The author starts by encouraging the reader to knock back several hard-core drinks at lunch. Acceptable choices include scotch, bourbon, martinis, or any drink served "neat." Wimpy choices included whiskey sours, mineral water, soft drinks, or anything blended or served with an umbrella. The author then suggests you only order "power foods," such as steak and broccoli, and avoid wimpy foods such as salads or fish. And the author actually *encourages* using sex as a weapon in business! (Now we at least know that the book was written long before the onslaught of sexual harassment suits preceding the era of corporate greed.)

The author summarizes a couple's actions (the man is hosting this lunch) as follows:

"Lunch affords many opportunities for flirtatious physical contact, always dangerous, but nevertheless effective if handled cautiously:

136

1. Brush her neck or gently lift her hair as you help her with her coat.

2. The moment she sits down next to you at the banquette, reach for her napkin and spread it on her lap.

3. In lighting her cigarette, if she does not reach for your hand, extend yours to steady *her* hand."

Do you think the author of this guide could have foreseen the world as it is today? The assumption that a businesswoman would be a smoker is so funny, as is the fact that most restaurants don't even *allow* smoking now! And if an executive tried to "reach for her napkin and spread it on her lap," he would likely get a backhanded slap across his face! I have had people guess that this must have been published before World War II. Actually, it was published a lot more recently than that—but the times have sure changed!

I know that corporate hanky-panky still happens, and will likely continue as long as boys will be boys and girls will be girls. There are plenty of metaphors about mixing business with pleasure to support that truth. I'm not your mother, but as an expert in business relationships, be wise and give lots of thought to any situation before crossing any lines. If you play it safe, you won't ever have to compromise your career.

Introductions

A sales rep, Laurie, once asked me a question that has probably crossed the mind of every account executive.

She was out to lunch with a *major* client (I believe it was her biggest account). As they were leaving the restaurant, she saw a table of her competitor's reps, all of whom were friends of hers, enjoying a business lunch with a client of their own. A few of them noticed her and waved at her to stop by and say "hi." She panicked and hurriedly ushered her client out to her car without stopping by the other table.

Laurie confessed that she was afraid for this table of "wolves" to meet her otherwise inaccessible client! She sheepishly laughed at herself when I reminded her of karma; I asked her if she knew who *she* missed out on being introduced to as a result of her fear of the others meeting *her* client. She didn't know. I have to agree that her fear was valid. Any one of that group would have seized the opportunity to hand Laurie's client his or her business card and follow up aggressively. That is why gaining an introduction can be such a wonderful thing—*most* of the time!

I'd like to think that in the same situation, we would each take the high road and stop by to say "hello," in spite of our fears. It is the polite thing to do and the proper way to handle such a situation. And because Laurie felt threatened, she could have shared that with her client afterward, even creating an inside joke between them. She could have told her client that it would be interesting to see which of these "wolves" was going to call the client first. Her client might be so put off by their predictability or assertiveness that Laurie would ultimately have nothing to fear. And, had she stopped by for an introduction, the very best way for any of the "wolves" to handle the situation would have been to invite Laurie *and* her client to join them and some of their clients for a fabulous dinner together—especially if that client was particularly inaccessible.

Adult entertainment

A new trend in business is taking clients to "gentleman's clubs" (a fancy name for strip clubs). One of my clients is a happily married man who works so many hours that he feels he doesn't get enough time with his wonderful wife and four kids. He once asked me, "Why would I want to spend even more time away from home, in an environment that I don't even care for?"

Forgive the comparison, but as with alcohol or dessert, you *usually* want to mirror your clients' behavior and, at the very least, show them acceptance. So what is my friend, or anyone in his situation, supposed to do? As we talked about his options, we became even more defensive of the poor *junior* executives who don't realize that taking clients to a gentleman's club could ultimately be a disaster. Yes, people go there all the time. Yes, you want to make your clients happy. However, you do *not* have to accompany them to any environment that makes you uncomfortable.

So what's the best way to handle it? If you think that an evening out with clients may end up at an adult club, and you do not want to participate, being prepared can save you. What's the best way to handle a situation when you are faced with *any* moral dilemma, but do not want to alienate your clients? Start by saying that it's against corporate policy. Say you could get fired. Then, in a move that is totally nonjudgmental, smile and tell your clients that you want to hear all about it in the morning. That is showing acceptance—as you decline to join them.

Never feel badly because you want to stand your ground. There was a story in the news recently of a guest at a strip club who got into a dispute with the bouncer over an $80 check. The man got belligerent and the bouncer threw him out. As a result of the fight, the ejected customer was permanently paralyzed. Alcohol, clients, and adult entertainment can be a very dangerous combination. I recommend that you learn when to call it a night.

Another associate of mine told me about a time when he was a junior executive and was out with his buddies from work. The beer was flowing and everyone was getting buzzed. One of the guys kept teasing their cocktail waitress, encouraging her to lift up her shirt for a tip. She eventually obliged and the boys roared their approval. My friend was very shy and uncomfortable. Now that he is older, he said he wishes he had stood his moral ground and left. It's a hard situation when you want to be liked and accepted, but you don't want to go along with what "everyone else" is doing. In business, when you want to show acceptance toward your clients, it's even more challenging.

Role-playing can help you to be prepared for such circumstances, although I'm sure circumstances will come up that no one can foresee. If you make the decision *now* to always stick to your principles, you won't find it so hard to do so when you actually face those challenges.

Acceptance

Let's consider how to make your clients feel comfortable when it comes to the actual meal. Imagine how your client would feel if you are health-conscious and on a tight program of working out and eating healthy. Your client is at least three sizes bigger than you are. Do you think that watching what you eat is going to make him or her feel comfortable? He or she is ordering lasagna and garlic toast while you are ordering a house salad with vinegar and lemon wedges. The odds are that he or she is going to feel guilty or fat, and at least a little uncomfortable.

I know what it's like to feel uncomfortable because I have been there—on both sides of the fence! When I am trying to lose weight and live a healthier lifestyle, business lunches can be challenging. This is especially true if I am dining with a client who is heavier than I am. I know how I felt when my size-four friend ate three bites of lunch and said she was just "so stuffed." Give me a break! I'm barely a size 10, and yet I felt *huge* in comparison! And it was not a good feeling.

If you are on a diet plan, you can always order a healthier meal without making a big fuss about it by getting your sauce or salad dressing "on the side," or by ordering vegetables instead of potatoes, and so on. No one will ever notice how you order, as long as you don't make a big deal out of it. I have learned by being on the "other side of the fence" what makes me feel comfortable, and have turned that around so that I can always put my clients at ease. If you are on a health plan, you can keep it to yourself and still enjoy a great lunch without intimidating your clients. Remember, too, that there

141

are plenty of excuses you can use for ordering lightly that won't affect how your client feels, including:

1. I'm still full from the *huge* dinner I ate last night.

2. My stomach is a little upset today, and I'm just not that hungry.

3. I have been craving a good bowl of soup lately, with some fresh bread!

4. I need to get more Omega-3 fatty acids, so I think I'll have the fish.

As you can see, none of these implies that you are making better or smarter choices than your client. They simply let you own your feelings and decisions.

Compare these suggestions with the following statements that accomplish the same thing, but may also succeed in making your client feel guilty or uncomfortable:

1. My size four pants feel so tight!

2. I need to lose 10 pounds by the time of my class reunion.

3. My personal trainer said that I could lose some weight by eating just veggies a few times a week.

Basically, anything you say may be interpreted as "I don't want to look like you," whether you mean it that way or not. If you are heavier, or even a lot thinner, than those around you, you may feel insecure about your appearance. People who are overweight know they are overweight. Some of us live to eat, and others eat to live. Whichever lifestyle you choose is up to you. However, you need to always be considerate of your client's position. If he or she enjoys eating a good meal more than a good walk on a treadmill, don't try to make him or her feel wrong or guilty for his or her choice, or boast about your own personal choices. Try to make it as unimportant as it *should* be as far as your relationship with them is considered.

On the other hand, if your client is the one on a diet, the last thing you want to do is tempt him or her with "evils" by ordering drinks, fried foods, or rich desserts to eat in front of him or her. Have you ever been on a diet when it seemed that everywhere you looked, all you saw was cake? It feels that way when you are trying to follow a plan.

If you are craving sweets or other temptations, you can always get something later, when you are alone. Or, if you know your client is on a health plan, you can grab a snack on your way to lunch. If you are still hungry after enjoying a light salad with your dieting client, there are convenience stores, fast-food chains, and ice cream parlors on nearly every corner. Be smart. Be supportive. If your client says he or she is trying to lose weight, say "Good for you. Me too!" And enjoy your charbroiled, boneless, skinless chicken breasts together! What you eat, and where you go afterward, is your own business.

How sweet it is!

I have certain clients who enjoy dessert. Therefore, I always take them to a restaurant that serves great desserts. I have a reputation for knowing which restaurants have the best pastry chefs or the best sweets. In fact, people call me to find out where the greatest desserts and pastries are! It is a mutual pleasure that I share with a lot of my clients. "Wait until you taste the white-chocolate bread pudding!" "They have an incredible molten lava chocolate cake here, and we can get it with a side of homemade vanilla ice cream!" We delight in finding new treats and treasures. If you are not a big dessert eater, it must be hard to comprehend the joy of finding great desserts. But if your client is a dessert lover, you should at least be aware of what is available, as well as be willing to share a great dessert with him or her. Even if you just take a bite or a nibble, you should encourage him or her to indulge if you know he or she will enjoy it.

Another suggestion is to offer to share dessert with your client. How bad can that be? At least it's not as many calories as eating an entire piece of cake by yourself! And, sharing a luscious dessert together can bond you and your client forever. You can always call at a later date and say, "I thought of you today. I found the most incredible chocolate crème brulee!"

Anytime you find some delectable dessert, it provides a perfect reason to call your client. Then, while you're discussing your latest cravings or findings, you will have an excuse to ask about business and to learn how things are going for him or her. It is also a great opportunity for you to invite him or her to lunch again. Sharing *any* common interest can help you to form a better relationship with people.

Profanity

On the list of *dos* and *don'ts*, profanity is definitely near the top of the list. There really is no need to use profanity in any business setting, and swearing can create tension or discomfort. Think about it; have you ever been around someone who displayed what your mother probably referred to as a "potty mouth"? Consider how it made you feel.

Does your client use profanity? If not, and you do, then beware. Your language will be offensive to him or her. It is never a good idea to be crass, or to swear gratuitously, or for shock value. But in business, you can offend the wrong person, and it can ultimately mean a huge loss for you— both personally and financially.

I believe the same thing applies to off-color stories and dirty jokes. Be careful—you might be overly confident about your relationship with a client and feel it is okay to tell a "dirty" joke. If your client tells you one that makes you blush, then you are probably on safe ground to recip- rocate. However, you'll do better to just laugh at his or her jokes and keep yours to yourself. You can never know exactly which joke might push the envelope too far, and in this case it's better to be safe than sorry.

Remember: You never want to make your clients un- comfortable, no matter what your personal opinion may be. A man I used to work with would never swear be- cause of his religion. We used to take clients golfing, and then go to lunch. He never wanted me to tell our guests that he was Mormon, because he knew that it might make them uncomfortable on the golf course. However, swear- ing can be quite common on the golf course, especially if a person's game isn't going as well as he or she had hoped for!

My coworker was putting our client's comfort before his. As much as it may have offended him to hear some cursing, he preferred putting the clients at ease for the sake of business. He never joined in, but I don't think anyone ever noticed. The clients always felt comfortable to be themselves, and enjoyed a great (or not-so-great!) round of golf with us. We just never made a big deal about the language.

The bottom line, always, is to make your clients feel comfortable. When in doubt, mentally switch places, and consider how you would feel if a situation was reversed. All of these choices—food, alcohol, topics of conversation— should be handled seemingly without notice. The business that you need to discuss, and the relationship that you are building, are always the most important things to be concerned with. Pay attention, and listen to your clients in order to avoid problems, and ensure long-lasting, successful relationships.

Courtesy

The most important behavior that you always want to exhibit during a meal with a client is plain, straightforward courtesy. Not every lunch you have is going to be perfect, even when have gone to great lengths to try to assure a smooth experience. Being rude toward a server is only going to make *you* look bad!

Shenandoah Merrick, a television executive in Las Vegas, told me that she was at a business lunch a few years ago with the chairman of the board of the American Heart Association and six other people who were attending a conference. When the waitress was bringing the group their drinks, the tray slipped and all of the drinks cascaded down the backs of the chairman and Shenandoah.

146

She said they laughed at the incident, dried themselves off, and kept on going. Shenandoah said she remembered being a little chilly, but that accidents happen. Wouldn't you love to be out with someone who could be so gracious under the circumstances?

Sometimes a steak arrives that is cooked too much or not enough. Other times, a waiter may forget something. How you respond to these setbacks is most revealing about the kind of person you are. Bad or challenging things happen to all of us. We are distinguished by how we handle them. Anyone can be gracious when things are running smoothly. Find someone who handles problems with grace, and you'll find someone exceptional—and someone people will want to do business with.

If you are trying to enjoy lunch with a client and your waiter is just dreadful, what's the best way to handle the situation? Perhaps the following story will offer a few suggestions.

My friend, Charles Clawson, once took a "big" client to a high-end restaurant. He sat for 15 minutes in disbelief as no one greeted them or stopped by their table. Charles finally walked up to the manager to ask for service.

When the waiter finally appeared, he snapped at Charles, saying, "It *wasn't* 15 minutes!" Charles knew that if he pursued this combative course that he might win the battle, but lose the war (he could possibly offend his client, or at the very least make him uncomfortable). So he let it slide.

The waiter knew he had taken too long to get to them and continued to act brusquely toward them throughout the entire lunch! When the waiter handed them the dessert menus, he scowled, "I would hate for you to have to get up and ask the manager for help again."

Charles said that if he hadn't been with his client, he certainly would have handled it differently. And he agreed that it was embarrassing to be put in that situation. In fact, he said that sometimes he feels his clients would actually *prefer* that he handle poor service a little more aggressively. If that's the case, and your clients urge you to take action, my best suggestion is to go over to the manager, away from your table of guests, to discuss the possibility of having someone else take care of you.

If you are served a nice lunch and your client's order comes out wrong, offer to share your lunch with him or her. Ask your server to suggest something else, or see if he or she can replace the order quickly. Try to laugh about it. Decide that you are not going to let this ruin your lunch. Remember that if you make a big scene, or if you are discourteous toward the server, it will only make you look bad. Tolerance is a trait that we all need to possess. You can ruin a relationship by exhibiting bad behavior at a business lunch. After that, no amount of kindness or service on your part will erase the damage that has already been done.

I can remember nearly every time that I have been with someone who was rude to a waiter or waitress. Once, about 20 years ago, I was enjoying some champagne with some of my associates. When my host ordered another bottle, the young waiter brought it out and started to pour it into our glasses—the same glasses we had just finished using. Our host told the waiter that it was a different wine.

The confused waiter double-checked the label and said, "No, it's the same wine that you ordered before." My host raised his voice a bit, and again told the waiter that it was a different wine. This went on for a few more minutes. The waiter was close to tears by the time my host *finally* asked for the manager. I was so uncomfortable, but I was this man's guest and really didn't think I should butt in—although now I definitely would.

The manager then explained to our waiter that because it was a different, *new* bottle of the *same* wine with the same label, that we should have been given clean glasses for it. That was so long ago, and I can still remember how embarrassed I felt for our waiter. How hard would it have been for our host to realize that the novice waiter didn't understand what the problem was, and that he should explain it to him? My host was rude and arrogant. It was obvious that the waiter did not understand what he was trying to say. And, although our host may have thought his actions made him look more knowledgeable, it only made him look bad in my eyes. I never went anywhere with him again. The thought of being with such an obnoxious, arrogant person is not inviting.

There are dozens of examples similar to that which I could cite here, but even *hearing* about them would make you uncomfortable! We need to conduct ourselves with grace, class, and consideration. And not just toward our clients, but toward everyone we deal with.

Graciousness

Along with being courteous, always remember to be gracious, friendly, and sociable. Never exhibit any kind of behavior that might reflect poorly upon you. My friend Charles remembered another lunch he attended, back when he was a summer accounting intern for a hospital management company in Houston. Everyone from the office went to the restaurant, and when lunch was over, one of the secretaries took everything off the table that wasn't nailed down! She literally *dumped* the container of sugar packets into her purse, gathered up all the breadsticks and leftovers, the salt and pepper shakers, and so on. He said it was as if she had tied up a tablecloth by its four corners and toted away the entire table!

Taking things off the table is always a no-no, with the exception of the leftovers you have for you or your clients. Be honest, be friendly, and—even though you are the host—always thank your guest for taking the time to join you.

Chapter 10

Subjects to Avoid

Never discuss your
health with a client—
unless it's good!

W hen meeting with a client, you should always avoid *all* offensive subjects. When in doubt, don't. If you have any confusion or uncertainty about what could be considered an offensive subject, just think about topics that guarantee a heated discussion, and you'll have your answer. I'm sure you will agree that to avoid the following subjects is just plain good advice.

⏱ Politics

Surely you've heard people debate opposing political sides for years. I'll bet that you received a *ton* of e-mails during the last election, with friends and neighbors trying to persuade you over to their way of thinking. Passion and emotions can run high when it comes to politics. Play it safe. You can say, "I haven't decided who I am going to vote for yet." But it's probably better to just say, "I'd rather not talk about that right now," and change the subject. You could even say something as innocent as, "I'm so *tired* of talking about it," and move on to something else. It's okay to change the subject as long as you do it tactfully enough that your client doesn't feel you don't care about his or her opinion. Never introduce politics as a topic, and always try to avoid political discussions with your clients.

⏱ Drugs

Having grown up in the drug culture of the 70s, I know that it was quite common for people in all walks of life to use recreational drugs. However, would you rather do business with someone who gets high, or would you rather work with someone who is straight? Do you think it depends which side of the fence you are on? Does it even matter? As you can see, your point of view can definitely color your client's point of view.

If you are both of the same opinion, then it is less important. But if you choose to "unwind" with a substance that is illegal, and your client does not, it could certainly affect your relationship if your client is aware of your behavior. Again, it's better to be safe than sorry. Some people have strong feelings about the use of drugs or alcohol, so try to keep your opinions to yourself.

Remember, too, that many people you know and work with may be in recovery for alcohol or drug addiction. If you are in a social setting, never insist that they join you in having a drink, as it can lead to uncomfortable situations—as I have experienced firsthand.

A former colleague of mine came up to me at an agency party last year. I was talking with one of the agency's account executives, who was in recovery for alcoholism. He didn't know that about the executive, and the first thing he said was, "Where's your drink?"

She replied, "I'm not drinking."

He responded by saying, "Aw, c'mon. You're more fun when you drink!"

I was mortified! My colleague is one of the most sensitive guys I've ever worked with. However, he probably had already consumed a drink or two at that point, and he wasn't aware of my client's situation. He had even been out drinking with this client in the past, so he didn't realize he was doing or saying anything wrong.

I asked him to get me a glass of wine just to get him to leave me alone with my client. Then, as soon as I could get him alone, I filled him in. He was very upset with himself. He said he was just caught up in the festivities, and it never occurred to him that the woman I was talking to had changed her lifestyle. We talked about it later, and I told him that when someone declines a drink, it is best to let it go. Never insist that someone have at least one drink, or suggest that they are not as much fun if they don't drink. We all have to admire anyone who chooses a healthier lifestyle, and need to respect his or her choices.

Abortion

Can you think of *any* topic that causes more controversy than abortion? What are the odds that you and your client are on the same side of the fence on this sensitive subject? Why would you ever bring it up? This is one topic to always avoid!

Sex

You are fighting with your spouse/live-in lover/boyfriend/girlfriend. Who wants to hear about that, unless you are perhaps relating a funny story that was

155

easily resolved? Money troubles, cheating, slacking, or problems with family are all great subjects for today's shock television programs. They don't, however, make good topics of discussion for a business lunch, unless you are talking about the television show itself.

⊙ **Your Health**

Earl Nightingale, one of the world's leading experts on success, once said, "Don't discuss your health (unless it's good), unless you are talking to your doctor." This is good advice. No one wants to hear about your aches and pains.

However, if your client has aches and pains, you should listen sympathetically. I like to share opinions and advice with my clients when they aren't feeling well. I always offer to bring chicken soup to anyone who is sick. I think it is really appreciated.

Remember to consider how you like to be treated when you are not feeling well, and then treat your clients the same way. People really appreciate it when you show them your caring, tender side. If someone is home for a couple of days, either from illness, or recovering from surgery, you can drop off magazines or a DVD. This is a great opportunity to get creative and really make a difference in his or her life, and your relationship with him or her.

I'm sure you're getting the idea. If you've ever gotten into a heated discussion over a controversial subject, then you know that two separate sides seldom come together. It is best to avoid any controversial topic during a business lunch. You'll know when you've made a mistake if you come away from lunch with an uneasy feeling in the pit of your stomach, and it's not the chili-cheeseburger that you're feeling. You may have touched on a topic you should have avoided. Feeling compromised is never good, particularly in a work environment.

Always practice discretion, especially in business

We are all going to make mistakes along the way. I remember when one of my male friends was going through a self-proclaimed "classic midlife crisis." His wife worked in our industry, and they were getting divorced. He was dating glamorous women from all around the world and was becoming a hot topic of gossip around town.

I was having a business lunch at Spago when I overheard some of the women who worked with his ex-wife discussing his love life. In spite of what was going on, it really wasn't their business to be discussing it, especially out in public. They were unaware that I was within earshot of them, hearing every word they had to say. I let them know that they had offended me and that they should not be discussing my friend.

When my friend felt he had made a mistake to get divorced, and realized he had just gone through a phase that had cost him dearly, he was able to make amends and get back together with his wife. Think about all of the things that happened to this couple and to their friends and family—all very personal. But because they worked in the same industry, and everyone had an opinion, it was far more difficult for them to get things back on track.

Did you hear why our manager got fired? He got caught messing with the auditor's figure.

Not surprisingly, I know another couple that went through a very similar situation, only it was even more complicated. The bottom line is that it is in everyone's best interest to maintain discretion about personal matters.

Lori Wilson, currently a district sales coordinator for Aflac Insurance, worked for a local business not too long ago. She recalls how the business had hired a manager to bring in more business and to help build relationships. Not only was the guy a "bunch of fluff" according to her, but he apparently had an agenda that wasn't going to benefit the company. He took Lori to lunch, where he tried to get her to open up. He told her that she should have some margaritas and enjoy herself.

She was very cautious with her new manager because of what had been happening internally at the company. "There was one sales rep that was constantly going into accounts I was working on and telling the clients that she was their new rep," Lori said. "This woman had a drinking problem, and almost lost one of our accounts when she kissed a client in front of his wife at a chamber mixer."

Lori said the situation between this new manager, the drunken sales rep, and the overall management of the company encouraged her to move on. She left a lot of commissions on the table at that point, just to get away. She knew she made the right choice when she decided to leave, rather than to compromise her ethics.

She summed up her experience by saying, "It's never worth any amount of money. I learned they later fired that manager. He did some bad things with the company's money."

People will talk, in spite of that little angel on their shoulder whispering into their ear to be quiet! Just try to think things through before you talk.

Knowing what to avoid, and how to behave, won't always guarantee that the wrong thing won't be said. How can that be? How can you slip and say the wrong thing, or go on about things you shouldn't? Here is a great comparison that will help to show how mistakes can happen. Perhaps being aware of this will help you to listen more carefully, and be more cautious, especially at business lunches.

In Las Vegas, casinos are built without windows and there is never a visible clock. Drinks are served free to gamblers at most of the casinos. These are conditions that are provided to create an atmosphere that is conducive to gambling. If you aren't aware of the time, or you've had one drink too many, you may forget yourself and your budget, as well as the fact that you may have told someone you'd be back in an hour. You *may* just end up spending a little more time or money than you had planned. These conditions are only slightly manipulative, and one could argue that they contribute to a more enjoyable experience in the casino.

You should set up the ideal business lunch with as much care as a casino gives to conducting business: You want your guest to feel comfortable and relaxed, totally at ease, and not looking at his or her watch.

Be aware, though, that mistakes may happen because you've attempted to create a mellow or fun atmosphere for your client's benefit. The odds are that you will become more relaxed, and not quite as "on guard" as you would be in an office or conference room, and you may well be enjoying yourself. You're having fun! You are getting along with your new "friend," and when he or she tells you something personal, it is very easy to reciprocate and share a personal "something" with him or her. You may be commiserating about your personal relationships, or something going on at the workplace.

However, imagine your client tells you that he or she thinks a coworker is stealing. You tell him or her you think one of *your* coworkers is on drugs. Sound dramatic? It is! And it is very unprofessional.

If someone tells you anything of a sensitive nature, remember my best advice: "Questions pull, statements push." If a client tells you they think a coworker is stealing, ask a question. "How do know?" "Can you be sure?" "What are you going to do about it?" "Did you tell anyone?" By doing this, the attention is directed away from you. It is your client's situation and problem—you are merely lending a friendly ear.

But sharing your office or business problems with a client could leave you (and your company) open to scrutiny and judgment by your client. Even though the client may *love* you, if he or she loses confidence in your company for any reason, it will ultimately come back to haunt you. Always keep your wits about you. It may sound trite, but it is great advice, especially with regard to business meetings. Don't commiserate when work is challenging.

Talk to your friends, family, a business consultant, or a counselor if you find yourself facing serious problems at work. Never share these problems with clients, no matter how well you think you know them.

Here's one final bit of advice about discretion in the workplace (or should I say "outside" the workplace?) You never know who is listening. I remember when my sister and I used to go to work with my father—back when he had an office on the 19th floor of the Illuminating Building in downtown Cleveland. It could be a long elevator ride up or down, especially when you are a child with boundless energy.

Each time my sister and I boarded the elevator, he put his finger to his mouth, reminding us to remain quiet. How simple and lasting that lesson became. It would be wonderful if everyone had learned that lesson by the time they became adults, but that's apparently not the case! Consider what happened to my friend, Kathy, when she was the vice president and branch manager of a local bank in Las Vegas.

Kathy told me what happened to her when some reported improprieties had come to surface about another bank employee—her senior manager—who was on vacation at the time. "With no notice, her superior—my regional manager—flew into town and scheduled meetings with each of the branch managers at a couple of local restaurants," said Kathy.

"The breakfast meetings were at IHOP," she explained, "and the lunch meetings were at Z-Tejas, a very popular southwestern-style restaurant in the heart of the business district. I was about eight months pregnant at the time, and was filled with anxiety about going to this meeting, the topic of which I was not told ahead of time. When I walked into the restaurant, I immediately spotted my regional manager sitting at a booth in the main dining area with the director of human resources (who had apparently just flown in from New Mexico). I almost fainted as thoughts whirled in my head about what was going to happen. I remember wondering if I was going to be promoted (not likely) or if something was seriously wrong (much more likely)."

"For the next hour I was publicly interrogated, questioned, grilled, and finally brought to tears—in the middle of Z-Tejas! Just months earlier, I had managed a branch for this bank within walking distance of this restaurant. Who knows who may have been within earshot? This restaurant was frequented by my clients and business associates. I was too distraught to see who may have been there that day, but I'm sure that there were witnesses who knew me. It was, by far, the lowest point in my career, not to mention a serious infraction by the bank (which could have led to legal action on my part). By being publicly embarrassed, I lost a lot of respect for a boss—a boss for whom I had little respect to begin with."

Remember that one of the criteria I listed for choosing a restaurant is a private room for meetings, as well as for detailed presentations. In spite of the fact that Kathy's boss's meetings were scheduled at the last minute, it would have only taken a few phone calls for her management to secure a restaurant with a private room. How little thought went into the choice of location for this dirty deed?

If you find yourself in charge of a serious lunch meeting, pick up the phone (or check your list of favorite restaurants for a business lunch), and find a restaurant with a private room. Don't risk being overheard by other clients, your competition, or anyone else who doesn't need to know your business.

Chapter 11

Knowing When to Stop Talking, Eating, and Selling

Stop eating when everyone else stops eating.

Stop talking

Let's consider again that "questions pull and statements push." Ask the right questions, and by the time lunch is finished, you should have accomplished what you set out to do—whether you are just establishing a relationship or presenting a proposal. Asking questions about your client's business, the climate of your industry, plans for the future, and other fact-finding queries should have helped you to establish common ground with your clients, and clue you in as to how you can best serve them. Once the business is taken care of, let go.

When I meet clients at a restaurant, I will usually finish up my proposal by letting them know that if they have to get back to the office, they can go as soon as we are done with lunch. As I mentioned briefly in Chapter 7, I don't want clients to feel that they have to hang around while I take care of the check (if I haven't taken care of it already). Sometimes my guests are grateful—they will check the time and agree that they should be going. Other times they will say they are okay—that they have more time to spend at lunch. It really depends on what they have waiting for them back at the office. If you established your time frame when you were seated, you will know if they are in a hurry or not.

You never want them to be looking at their watch while you have them "cornered," insisting that you need just a few more minutes to finish. You've had lunch already! Why would you wait until the last minute to get what you came for? Be aware. Pay attention to your client's body language and look for signs that they are getting anxious to wrap things up. And when you notice these signs, stop talking.

Stop eating

You need to stop eating when everyone else stops eating. If you want to get the rest of your meal to take with you, there's nothing wrong with that. But if you are still munching away long after your guests have put down their forks, then either you did all the talking through lunch (which is a mistake), or you are just not keeping up.

Pay attention throughout lunch, and if you see that everyone is eating faster than you, ask more questions— let them do some of the talking—and catch up! Besides, how are you going to learn anything if *you* are doing all the talking? Try to make it so that you all finish at the same time. Keeping tabs on everyone's plate will also tell you if you are eating too fast. Pace yourself.

The worst-case scenario that might cause diners to finish at different times is when the lunch order comes out wrong, and everyone in your party is served at the same time—except one person. Whether it is you or one of your clients, it is awkward to be the only one at the table who is still eating. I've had that happen even when I'm simply out to lunch with friends and it is uncomfortable. With a client, it is even more unsettling. As I mentioned in Chapter 9, a great way to overcome awkward moments when you are each served at a different time is by sharing your meal. "Why don't we split this and then, when you get your meal, we can share that, too." Sounds pretty nice, don't you think? Or, if your client chooses to wait for his or her meal and you should finish first, you can order coffee or tea, or something you can "play" with while your guest is finishing his or her lunch, so that he or she is not made to feel self-conscious about eating alone. If you can, eat slowly so there is a greater likelihood of finishing at the same time.

If it is your lunch that comes to the table late, so late that everyone else is finishing up, take it with you rather than eat alone. Just tell your guests that you have to get back to the office, and you'll finish it later.

Stop selling

Whether you have chosen to present a proposal while waiting to be served, or if you used your lunchtime to learn as much as possible (in order to help you present after your meal), the time will come when you have to stop selling. You will have reviewed the options and benefits. A proposal will either come to a definite conclusion (in other words, it will be signed at lunch) or it will enter the wheels of progress, where you learn that it will need to be shown to the manager, boss, owner, committee, client, and so on. Either way, you will have done your job.

Know when to stop and wrap things up. You can always ask a question: "What do you think of this proposal?" If your client says he or she loves it, then you've done your job well. Stop selling! Do what you need to wrap things up and plan your next move or arrange your next meeting.

Your client may have some objections or problems with the information or proposal as you have presented it (which can happen, even when you have taken every precaution to assure that it was perfect). Things can change quickly in business, so be prepared. By the time lunch is over, you should know exactly what has changed, so you can either amend the proposal you have or offer to bring a revised version to his or her office later (one that is tailored to what he or she is looking for). For example, you could say, "Now that I know what it is that has changed, I can rework these numbers, plans, projections, and so on, for you. I'm so glad we had this chance to get together so that I could learn firsthand exactly what you are looking for!" Of course you should put such a statement in your own words, and be as appreciative as possible that he or she shared so much of his or her time and knowledge with you.

When you are booking your business lunch date, try to get as much information as possible, to avoid having a less-than-perfect presentation. I know it can sometimes be difficult to find out all of the information you will need to put together the ultimate proposal. But you should be able to discover enough information about what your client wants so that you can "wow" him or her at the table.

When your lunch is nearly finished, move on to the final topic, which is likely to be scheduling your next meeting with your client, or covering what you need to do next to complete your sale. I have heard many stories about a sale that was made—only to be lost because the salesperson didn't know when to quit. Try not to be that person!

The biggest sale

If the main purpose of your lunch date is to build a relationship, and you do not have a specific proposal to present, you might not think you have anything to sell. Think again. You are *always* selling yourself, your company, your services, and your commitment to your client. And *that* kind of selling *never* stops! You should possess so much enthusiasm for what you do that you never stop being excited about your work. I'm not saying don't ever take a day off. I *am* saying that you should always remember that *you* are your primary product, and your clients have to buy you before they buy anything you may be selling.

If you don't like where you are, then make changes. There are so many exciting opportunities in our world to work with great people and to do good work. If you don't feel that you could sell yourself, or your company, 24 hours a day, seven days a week, then it might time for you to make a change.

Chapter 12

There Is No Free Lunch: Settling the Check Discreetly

Never pay for a
business lunch
with cash!

Settling the check discreetly can be an art in itself! Taking pains to handle the check before lunch will always prove to be the best way. There are many ways to impress your guests with a little thoughtfulness and preparation. In our busy workdays, however, it's not always possible to beat the clock. Even if you arrive at the restaurant at or about the same time as your guests, there are still ways to pay for your meal that will assure a nice finish.

Sometimes it is as easy as excusing yourself to visit the restroom. While away from the table, flag down your server and ask to settle things while you are out of sight from your clients. *Never* leave to go to the restroom after lunch and before the check comes, unless you are going to find your waiter on the way! It could give your client the opportunity to pay for the lunch, which is the last thing you want to have happen. Be aware of everything going on around you and make sure that you are the one who will be picking up the check!

If the waiter brings the check to the table, *always* pay with a credit card. You don't want to be shuffling through your cash and counting bills. Paying with cash can create a "let's all chip in" type of atmosphere. Your guests may feel uncomfortable. They will likely offer to pay or at least to "get the tip." A credit card is direct. It says, "I've got it." When your waiter returns the credit card slip for a signature, add at least a 20 percent tip, sign the form, and take your copy of the receipt. Make as little to do of the transaction as possible.

Don't *ever* ask your client about the check total, so that you will know how much to tip. This can be perceived as a ploy (used by rude people to make their guests aware of how much they are spending on them)—and it is not polite. If you can't read a check without your glasses, then make sure you always have your reading glasses with you! I know that I do not enjoy being made to feel obligated or indebted, and I'm sure clients do not, either. It is *not* a good way to impress someone or to do business. The menus today have prices on them, and I'm sure your clients will know how much you are spending on them (and will appreciate your handling the check discreetly).

Never get caught being cheap!

My friend, Barbara Dempsey, has worked in Las Vegas as a media buyer for as long as I can remember. She told me about an experience she had with an account executive that I found shocking.

As a media buyer, she was frequently taken to lunch by radio and TV sales reps for the main purpose of trying to get her to buy advertising from them. She accepts this fact, and usually goes to lunch only with the people she likes spending time with. Still, she has made an occasional exception to her rule.

"Once, a male rep wanted to take me to lunch at a very nice Japanese restaurant," she told me. "He pitched. I listened, and ultimately declined for the client in question. He asked for the check, and when it came, he acted embarrassed and frantically looked for his wallet. He had scrip ("fake" money issued by the restaurant—a common trade practice for advertising) to pay for the lunch, but no money to pay for the tip. I happily obliged.

"After six months had passed, he asked me out to lunch again. We did the same dance when the bill arrived, and would you believe it, he once *again* did not have his wallet and asked me to pay for taxes and tip. I did, wondering whether, if I had bought the station he represented, would I have been asked to pay, or was he in early dementia? Too coincidental!

"Another two months go by," Barbara continued, "and I am having lunch with a few other media buyers. This gentleman passed by our table and one of the buyers said, 'Gee, is he alone?' We all agreed that he was, and she said, 'Hope his memory has improved. I had lunch with him last week and he forgot his wallet, and he didn't have enough scrip to pay the rest of the check and the tip.' The table immediately fell into uncontrollable laughter—*all* of them had experienced the same exact circumstances with this 'cheap' salesperson."

Barbara added a moral to her story: "Don't think competing media people don't talk. Don't be such a cheapskate, or at least change your modus operandi with different people." She finished by saying it wasn't so much that they minded paying here and there, but rather the deception that she deplored.

So, remember: Don't be cheap. Aside from the fact that your waiters and waitresses work primarily for tips, you will only succeed in making yourself look bad. And it's not just media people who talk amongst themselves.

Sorry. This latest round of budget cuts is really taking the fun out of business lunches!

The circles of any given business can be very small. You will never live down a reputation for being cheap.

And if you happen to have a trade agreement with a restaurant, or you are using scrip or a certificate, show up early and pay for your check *before* your guests arrive. Talk to your waiter and give him or her enough to cover the check. Then either arrange to stop back by to handle the change and the tip, or cover yourself beforehand. Either way, when you have finished your lunch and taken your guest back to his or her office or car, he or she will be impressed that you handled everything so well. And never, ever use a coupon when taking a client out to lunch! No matter what the circumstances, or how friendly you are with your clients.

I remember being invited out to lunch by a printer's rep who was trying to get my business. I had known Al professionally for a few years but had never done business with him directly. He had faxed me some prices, and we had spoken on the phone. He was going to be in town and he suggested we rendezvous for lunch.

We met at a The Palm and enjoyed a great conversation. We discussed business and pricing, and what he was going to be able to do with the project on which I was working. Finally the check came. And it sat there. And sat there. And sat there. Al made no sign of reaching for it.

I was this man's client, he invited me to lunch, *and* he was trying to sell me something!

I finally reached for the check and said, "Well, let's see what we've got here."

I started to feel better when Al reached for his wallet. But the feeling didn't last long.

When he pulled his wallet from his back pocket, he said, "Here, let me get the tip." I was stunned! I could not believe that this man invited me out for a business lunch—with the purpose of trying to sell me his products and services—and he let me get the check!

I stuffed my American Express card in the check cover and said, "Never mind. I've got it." Do you think he got my business?

Anyone who orders from a menu has an idea of the prices. All it takes is a little grace and a bit of class to settle a bill without much ado. If anything on a check ever stands out as a gross or obvious error, you can mention it, of course, or you can always come back later to settle any discrepancy. It is better to handle it when you are not in the presence of your client.

I'm sure you have felt uncomfortable at times when certain people have paid for your meal. You'd rather pay for it yourself than deal with that awkward or uncomfortable feeling. Now imagine if you were your client. How would you like your representative to handle taking *you* out to lunch? It's nice to be treated like royalty, or at least as though you are important. Remember this, and always treat your clients as though they are the most important people in your life, because for that lunch date, they are!

Plan, in order to "floor your guests"!

Another way you can settle the bill discreetly is by going to the restaurant and paying for lunch *before* your lunch date. I remember when I first read Harvey Mackay's book, *Swim With the Sharks Without Being Eaten Alive*

(Ballantine Books, 1996). He suggested handling the bill in advance. Mackay said you will "floor your guests" when you say, "Let's go. Everything's been taken care of."

Successful business executives have done this for years, and anyone who has ever tried it will tell you how much fun it is to do. I have handled checks in this manner for birthday lunches, and other special occasions, and it really makes a great impression.

Choose a place that you frequent and that you trust. Talk to the host or hostess about your intentions. You can give him or her your credit card ahead of time to use when you are done with your meal. If possible, meet the person who will be your server, and tell him or her what you hope to accomplish. Explain that you will include a 20 percent tip (or more), and that you will stop by after lunch to retrieve your credit card and receipt.

Then, when you are done with lunch, simply ask your guests if they are ready to go. They will usually ask about the check. As Mackay suggested, tell them it's already been taken care of. Make sure to thank your server or hostess on the way out. Paying for a meal ahead of time is a very subtle tactic, but it will be a very memorable move.

If subtle isn't your style, and you want to impress your clients, you can be more flamboyant (depending on your industry, and what you are hoping to accomplish). For example, my friend Marty (who lives here in Las Vegas), was entertaining some guests in Los Angeles. Marty's clients chose the location and told him where to meet them. He stopped by the restaurant about an hour before the reservation was scheduled, and he plied everyone at the restaurant (including the bartender, his waiter, and the manager) with $20 bills. He asked the staff to act as if he was a regular. He also had hired a limousine, and then waited in it while watching the door to the restaurant.

When his clients showed up, Marty's limo pulled up, and the driver opened the door for him to get out. His clients saw all of this and were, at the very least, a little impressed. Then they entered the restaurant together.

The manager came up to him, gave him a hearty handshake, and said, "Hey, Marty! Where the heck have you been? It's been a while since we've seen you here!" The waiter then asked Marty how his beautiful wife was doing. A similar scene occurred at the table when a bus boy asked about Marty's dog (by name!), and then the bartender sent over some drinks.

When everyone at the restaurant made a fuss over Marty, his clients weren't just impressed—they were puzzled. They asked him if he came to this restaurant very often. He told the truth, and said he'd been there only once before. His clients were absolutely floored. They thought, "Marty must know *everybody!*" It was even more impressive, considering he didn't live in Los Angeles.

Of course, Marty had also prearranged to pay for the check. His clients were so impressed with him that they immediately moved into negotiations with him on a new project (one they had previously felt might not have been within his area of expertise). He is still working with them.

Marty loves to do things that are "over the top" because he knows that taking extra care with his clients will result in increased business and stronger relationships. Anytime you get creative and apply yourself, you too will see outstanding dividends.

Chapter 13

You'd Be Surprised: Etiquette Essentials

Never push your plate away or stack your dishes.

Although I have touched upon some of the aspects of basic etiquette throughout this book, there are several points (especially those that pertain to dining), that you should know so that you will be totally confident and relaxed when take your clients to lunch. Some of the tips I'll offer you were responses to questions I have been asked in the past, and others involve stories that may make you say, "You've got to be kidding! Who doesn't know *that?*" Well, you'd be surprised! There are apparently many business executives working today who do not even know that it is impolite to talk with your mouth full!

So, let me first mention, "Don't talk with your mouth full of food!" And I probably need to add, "Don't chew with your mouth open." If you've made it in business without knowing these two rules, that's amazing. Some things seem so obvious. Talking with your mouth full would have to be one of the most important to remember, but that's just the start.

When you talk about etiquette, most people think you are referring to which fork goes where and what you should do with your napkin. The rules of etiquette are actually a blueprint for good manners. Dining etiquette is just a small part of the big picture. Sending thank-you notes, returning telephone calls, calling to RSVP, and many other behaviors that I have mentioned in this book are all a part of proper etiquette.

You should never be so intimidated by the rules as to pass up an opportunity to take a client to lunch. You should, however, be familiar with most of the basic rules, so that you will be self-assured enough to proceed. Some of the behaviors may seem old fashioned, but knowing what to do, or how to handle yourself in a social situation, will make a world of difference—especially when you are with others who are in the know.

The rules

Some of the rules of etiquette are very interesting, as you will learn, and many deserve to be repeated. There are a lot of *nevers* and *always* when it comes to any set of rules, so learn them once, and you're set for life! As I've said before, *always* make a reservation. It would be disastrous to show up at a restaurant with your client only to find out that the restaurant is full and cannot seat you.

When you first get to the restaurant and learn who will be taking care of you, you can discreetly hand your waiter your credit card. This will not only eliminate any awkwardness as to who will be paying for lunch when you are done with your meal, but doing so also tells your waiter that *you* are the host or hostess of this luncheon or meal. Your waiter will then look to you for cues throughout the remainder of the meal.

Once you are seated, pick up your napkin and place it on your lap. Do not make a big flapping gesture as if you were changing the sheets on a bed or snapping towels in a high school locker room! Simply unfold it slightly, and place it across your lap. If it is a large napkin, the fold should go toward you. (In some restaurants, the host or waiter who seats you will drape your napkin across your lap for you.) *Never* tuck your napkin into your shirt as though a bib. In addition, ladies should not use their napkins to remove lipstick.

Most importantly, remember that your napkin is not a substitute for bathroom tissue. If you should sneeze at the table, cover your mouth with your hand or a tissue. And if you have to blow your nose, excuse yourself and go to the restroom. You should *never* blow your nose at the table. Snorting is not acceptable, either. In fact, if you have to make any kind of noise that might interfere with someone else's lunch, you should excuse yourself from the table. If you need to excuse yourself anytime during the luncheon, place your napkin on your chair, or over the back of your chair, if you prefer. (Etiquette primarily dictates that you leave it on your chair. However, I know a marketing consultant, Andrew Klebanow, who refuses to do so. He believes that draping it on the back of your chair is more hygienic—and I really can't argue with the logic of that. Andrew is a marketing genius, with a background in food and beverage, so I yield to his expertise on this subject.) When you return to your seat, your waiter should have refolded your napkin and placed it alongside of your place setting. (Andrew also said that in a better restaurant, your waiter should *replace* your napkin with a fresh, clean one. After all, who wants to wipe their mouth with a napkin that a waiter has just handled extensively?) When you are done eating and ready to leave, place your napkin, slightly folded and clean-side up, to the left of your plate.

If you are meeting clients for the first time, offer them one of your business cards after you are seated. Make sure it is face-up and in good condition. I have been offered the business card of a new acquaintance at lunchtime, and I usually will keep it in plain view on the table until lunch is over, just to make sure that I remember a new guest's name. This is particularly helpful if your client brings along an associate that you have never met or worked with before. Otherwise, you should make it a point to know who your guests are and memorize their names, job titles, and any other information you can learn about them, *before* the lunch meeting. This will make starting a casual conversation easier. When you are done with lunch, remember to take your guest's card with you when you go.

After you have been seated, you might want to offer your client the choice of when he or she would like to discuss business. As I mentioned in Chapter 7, most people prefer to eat first, as this gives you a chance to establish a rapport with your client, help you get to know them a little better, and will helps you to be prepared to talk business with them after the meal.

You should *always* excuse yourself to the restroom if you need to take medication, or if you want to use dental floss or a toothpick. Years ago I had a European girlfriend, Elizabeth, who used to pick her teeth at the table, using a toothpick with one hand and holding her other hand over her mouth to conceal her actions. She did it with such a flourish that I used to question whether using a toothpick at the table really was improper! All of my friend's movements were very graceful, and even though it is, in fact, improper to use a toothpick at the table, I felt that she could get away with it. But I also felt that she was possibly the only exception. The rest of us should *always* leave the table to attend to our dental hygiene or to reapply makeup. Never use sinus spray or eye drops at the table, either.

During my first year in advertising sales, I called on a nasty car dealer who took delight in making others feel uncomfortable. From politically incorrect jokes, to insulting someone's birthplace or religion, you could always count on him to say or do the wrong thing. (If you happened to notice, you would see him chuckle each time he stepped on someone's toes.) He was, however, on my client list, and I needed to call on him.

I remember trying for weeks to get an appointment with him before finally succeeding. There I was, sitting in his office for our 2 p.m. appointment. I stared in disbelief as he took out his dental floss and proceeded to clean his teeth in front of me—while I was discussing a proposal! Sizeable chunks of food were flying across his office, and I know he was laughing inside at my disgust.

Knowing what I do now, I'm sure he loved the fact that he upset me. He apparently had shared the story with a mutual friend, reveling in just how much fun he had by flossing his teeth in front of me. If that situation were to happen to me today, I would excuse myself from the meeting and have the account reassigned to someone less sensitive.

As a salesperson or business professional, we should *always* try to put ourselves in someone else's shoes to see if what we are saying or doing could be offensive, especially when it comes to working with members the opposite sex. Men need to be aware that some things that wouldn't faze them might be very offensive to a woman.

Bill Jelen, founder of MrExcel.com, once shared one of his experiences that perfectly illustrated how certain actions can be perceived quite differently by women and men. Though his story could have found its way into my next chapter on job interview lunches, the fact that it illustrates a complete breach of proper etiquette demands that I share it with you here. Please remember that if you ever find yourself at a job interview luncheon, consider the following as what *not* to do!

When Jelen worked at Telxon, he and a female co-worker took a job candidate to lunch.

"The candidate was sharp, but he made a major mistake," Jelen explained. "He took the knife out of the mustard jar, spread mustard on his sandwich, licked the knife, and put it back in the mustard jar. This so annoyed my co-worker, she never listened to another word the guy said during the interview. The candidate did get the job, but my coworker despised the guy from that day forward—all from the reflex reaction of licking the mustard off the knife."

Jelen and I agreed that this is something that one *might* do at home. But you should *never* forget your manners when you're out. Was licking the mustard knife a "guy thing"? Some men might not think things such as this are a big deal (although I'm sure that many men would be just as offended as Bill's coworker). Be aware of these differences, especially when you are out with clients. Be on your best behavior and treat your clients accordingly.

We all need to be tuned in to our differences and deal with them positively. Just as men have special issues they need to be aware of, so do women. A woman's flirtatious behavior will only net trouble for her. Don't compromise

yourself by initiating blue humor or by dressing sugges-
tively. Be responsible about your behavior, and send a
professional message. You are less likely to encounter a
problem if you act in a purely professional manner. If anything, being a woman should become a nonfactor, as the
men who you take to lunch realize that you are there for
business.

After you have gotten to know someone better, you
both might be inclined to relax a little. In a new relationship, however, it is always better to play it safe and pay
special attention to your words and gestures, so that no
one will ever get the wrong idea about your intentions.

On a less dramatic note, women should be aware of
where they place your handbag when at a business lunch.
It is improper, as well as risky, to hang it over the back of a
chair. You should set it on the floor just under your chair,
being careful that any shoulder straps or handles are not
going to trip your waiter or passersby. Because some ladies feel that it is bad luck to place a handbag on the floor,
many formal restaurants have petite footstools designed
exclusively for ladies to set their handbags upon. But in a
contemporary restaurant, if there is an empty chair at the
table, that may be used as a convenient place to put a
handbag.

Pay attention to your posture at a business lunch, or at
any dining or cocktail function. If you are standing up at a
cocktail party, stand up straight. Do not ever lean against
a wall or a post. When seated at a table, keep your feet
flat on the floor. It is okay to cross your legs at the ankles,
but if you try to cross your legs at the knees, you may
inadvertently kick your guest. You should also keep your
shoes on.

Whenever I see someone kicking his or her shoes off in a restaurant, I am reminded of a story that my uncle, Lenny Kalter, once told me.

Lenny was a bar manager in Las Vegas many years ago. At the time, a major Hollywood actor/singer used to come into the restaurant for business lunches when performing in town. Apparently this actor was in the habit of wearing tennis shoes without socks. Sweaty feet and rubber soles baked in the desert heat create an extremely unpleasant foot odor!

Lenny said this performer used to kick off his shoes while he was having his lunch or dinner. He would invariably empty the room! The guests around him for a 20-foot radius would be so repelled that they would have to leave! Unfortunately, this actor was so well-respected, that no one wanted to offend him by saying anything. I think about his stinky feet whenever I see him on television! Now *that's* a lasting impression, and a bad reputation that none of us in business would ever want to have. Keep your shoes on!

I have been out to lunch on occasion when my female guests will kick off their shoes, most likely because those high heels start to hurt around midday. This is yet another special consideration for the ladies. Although you may not have smelly feet, if you kick off your shoes you are going to have to reclaim them at some point. That can lead to scuffling about under the table. Try to avoid any behavior that could possibly lead to an awkward situation.

I think most of us learned as children to *never* put our elbows on the table. But just what *is* acceptable? Hands and forearms are—that's it. There is never a reason to put your elbows on a table. It expresses fatigue, discontent, and, worst of all, boredom. Not exactly the message you want to send to your client! If you are squeezed into a booth next to another guest or associate, try to keep your elbows close to you so that you do not bump into your neighbor. If you are left-handed, try to sit so that your left side is at the end of a table. That way, you won't disturb the guest who is seated to your left. And for those times when you are not eating, and are in doubt as to what to do with your hands, you can always fold them in your lap.

The actual meal

When it comes to the actual meal, many people don't know when to begin eating. Proper etiquette dictates that if the entrées are cold, diners should wait until everyone else has been served. If the entrées are hot, then it is correct to begin eating when you are served. However, if your client has not yet been served, you should either wait until he or she has been served (even if it means yours might cool off significantly) or offer to share your entrée with him or her until his or hers arrives. (This is one of the differences between *basic* etiquette, and *business* etiquette—which puts your client's needs first.)

Of course, if your client says that you should go ahead and begin, then feel free to do so. I always prefer to share my entrée if I have been served but my guest has not. We've all been through the scenario where the food comes out at different times or, worse yet, there is something wrong with someone's meal. When in doubt, it is best to wait. Try to always let your client lead, and take the first bite.

Speaking of bites, my brother, Barry, told me about a woman with whom he once had lunch. She kept taking such big bites of her food that it made having a conversation with her nearly impossible. Barry said she would take a huge bite of her food, and then try to talk to him, either with her mouth full, or hurrying to chew the mass and swallow it so she could talk to him. Of course, she would then take *another* big bite! He said it was so annoying! Remember to always take small bites, especially if you are at a business lunch. You might be asked a question (or otherwise be called on to speak), and you will want to be ready.

When it comes to understanding the place settings, knowing several simple tips will help you to feel comfortable and assured. Food plates, such as bread and butter, go to the left, and glasses for beverages go to the right of your main plate. At nearly every business lunch I've ever attended, no one has ever seemed to know which bread and butter plate is his or her own.

Michael Levine, affectionately known as "Cookie Man" (from when he worked at a cookie company), told me about the *b* and the *d*—which is a great method for remembering how to find your bread-and-butter plate or water glass. With your right hand, make an "okay" sign, with your thumb and index finger forming a circle and your other fingers straight up. If done correctly, you will have not only formed an "okay" sign, but also the letter "d" (lowercase). Now, when you are seated at a table, do that with both hands in front of you. They will look like a lower case "b" and "d." Simply remember that "b is for bread" and "d is for drink," and you'll never again have to question which bread plate or drink is yours. Another way to remember is to think of BMW (bread, meal, and water) left to right on the table setting before you.

If you are dining at a high-end restaurant, a small knife called a butter spreader will be placed across the bread and butter plate. Your water glass, wine glass, soda glass, or coffee cup will always be to the right, above your dinner plate. Any silverware that is above your plate is for dessert, whether it is a fork or a spoon. Your napkin will either be to the left of your plate, on your plate, or in your water goblet. Also to the left, you will find your forks. When wondering which utensil to use, remember to always start from the outside and work your way in toward the plate. The salad fork is to the far left, then the dinner fork, then the plate...and on the right side of the plate, you will find the knife next to the plate, and a soup spoon on the outside right. Imagine they are all lined up like little soldiers, waiting to help you through your meal. If you are not having a salad, your waiter should remove the salad fork when he serves your entrée. But if he doesn't, know to use your larger fork, the dinner fork, for your entrée. If you are ordering a steak, your waiter should bring you a steak knife before you are served. And if you have coffee after your meal, your waiter should bring you a teaspoon with your coffee.

If your work requires that you take clients out frequently for formal dinners, then I would recommend that you pick up a book on etiquette to familiarize yourself with all of the potential choices that you may have to make. It can be intimidating if you have never seen a formal setting before, and your guests may be looking to you to see which utensil to use first. Because of that, it is imperative that *you* know how to proceed. A formal place setting may contain some of the following: individual salt and pepper shakers, a place card or menu card, up to five goblets (water, champagne, white wine, red wine, and sherry), a fish fork and knife, a cocktail fork (for shellfish appetizers), and a salad knife, as well as the dinner knife. Most of the time, though, you won't go wrong by starting with the utensils on the outside of your place setting and working your way in.

A formal table will be set according to what will be served, so it will be hard to make a mistake in such an instance.

If you are having a beverage in a stemmed glass, always hold it by the bowl, so you don't risk spilling it. The only exceptions to this are when you are drinking white wine or champagne. Holding the bowl of a goblet in that case might cause the chilled wine to become warm.

It is polite to taste your food *before* you add seasoning. Your waiter will usually offer fresh ground black pepper for salads and soups. Even if you are the type of person who always salts your food or puts Tabasco on your eggs or steak, or if you know that you like a lot of pepper on your food, it shows good manners to taste your food first. Besides, tasting your food first will give the impression that you know what you're doing and indicate that you have a sensitive palate. Also, you should always keep the salt and pepper together on a table. If someone asks you to pass the salt, you should pass the salt and the pepper together. Just picture them together, and keep them together—a happy couple.

When eating soup, you should always "eat away" from yourself. If you don't know what this means, I'll explain. It would look terrible if you were trying to get your soup into your mouth as fast as possible. You would probably lean over the bowl and move the soup spoon back and forth in a fast motion between the bowl and your mouth.

To imagine what "eating away" means, imagine if you were feeding your soup to the person across the table from you. You would fill your spoon with soup, moving your spoon from your side of the bowl to the far side of the bowl; lightly touch it on the far side of the soup bowl to catch any drops, as if you were going to offer it to your guest. That is the motion that you should use when eating soup, except that after you dab your spoon on the far side of your bowl, you would then bring the spoon up to your mouth.

Eating your soup in this manner will not only slow you down, but will also lessen the likelihood of spilling any soup on yourself. When you are finished with your soup, place your spoon on the plate beneath your bowl, so your waiter will know you have finished.

When it comes to eating your entree, there are two different styles, American and European (also referred to as English and Continental), and either is acceptable.

The American style involves holding your fork in your left hand, tines facing down, and holding your knife in your right hand, with your index finger along the handle. Once you cut your food, (one piece at a time!), lay the knife along the top of the plate, cutting side facing you. Switch the fork, with the food on it, into your right hand and put the food in your mouth. It seems as if it's quite a production, and it involves excessive handling of your silverware. But we have become quite accustomed to seeing this and eating this way in America, and most people will hardly give it a thought.

If you prefer, you can adopt the Continental method, which is similar to the American method, except that once you cut your food, you just bring your fork up to your mouth and eat the bite. It's pretty simple! Always remember, also, that once you have used a piece of silverware that it should *never* be placed back on the table again. It should remain completely on the plate. When you are done with your course, place your fork and your knife together, diagonally across your plate so that your server will know that you are finished.

Here is another important piece of advice with regard to your utensils: Never take a taste of someone else's food directly from his or her plate. It is rude in any case, but is especially wrong to do at a business lunch! You might be comfortable doing this with good friends, or with a member of your family, but remember that this is a business lunch, and that kind of familiarity is uncalled for.

If your guest asks you if your entrée is good, or vice versa, you can exchange tastes. You can cut off a piece of whatever you are having and place it on his or her plate or bread and butter plate, so that he or she may enjoy a taste of what you are having, and he or she may do the same for you. Remember to make the offer before you begin to eat, so that you are cutting his or her piece with clean utensils. You might even want to be the first to offer a taste of your entrée, although it would be wrong to ask your client for a taste of what he or she ordered if he or she does not offer.

Judi Moreo, an expert in the areas of communication, customer service, and diversity, shared a story with me that I found to be incredible. This was much worse than taking a bite off of someone else's plate. She was speaking at a seminar in Denmark along with a blind gentleman (who was speaking about overcoming adversity) and another man who owned about 30 car dealerships around the world (who was giving a talk about success).

At lunchtime, the blind gentleman was seated between Judi and the car dealer. They were served prime rib, and Judi said the car dealer's slice of meat was apparently on the rare side. The car dealer actually switched plates with the blind gentleman, without saying a word to him, or asking his permission. He must have thought that because the man was blind that he was also unaware of movement around him! As he did so, the blind gentleman leaned over to Judi and said, "I guess he thought *my* lunch looked better."

Can you imagine? The blind gentleman was able to resolve the situation with the help of his waiter. I was stunned when she shared this story with me, as was she when she witnessed it firsthand! It's hard to imagine anyone showing such rude behavior—especially someone who was lecturing on success! Switching plates, without a doubt, is a much greater offense than taking a bite off of someone else's plate.

Certain food items require special attention. I've already talked about the proper way to eat soup, but what about a piece of bread to go with it? If a bread basket is placed in front of you, you should offer it to your guests first. If the bread basket holds a loaf of bread, and it is lined with a napkin, you should try to use the napkin to hold the bread so that you can break off a piece for yourself without touching anyone else's bread with your hands, if possible. If there are more than two of you at the table, it is proper to pass the bread to your right. If you notice that the bread basket is empty, ask your waiter to bring more for your table. If you are at a restaurant that serves warm bread when you are seated, and the bread has become cold, it is fine to ask for some fresh, hot bread when your waiter serves your meal, or at any other time during the meal. If there is a butter dish for the table, do not ever butter your bread from it directly. Instead, you will want to serve yourself by putting some butter on your own bread and butter plate. Take the butter spreader from the butter dish or your own butter spreader if there isn't one on the butter dish, and put some butter onto your bread and butter plate. Then butter your bread from there.

You should never butter your entire piece of bread at once, as though you were making a sandwich! Always tear off one or two bites of bread from your larger piece, and butter that piece only. Make sure that you keep the buttering action over your bread and butter plate, not over your entrée plate. Your bread and butter plate is always going to be to the left of your entrée plate, and it should be comfortable for you to deal with your bread over that plate. It is also impolite to dunk or drag your bread through sauces, unless the dish is designed that way (for example, with infused olive oil for dipping, or with a French Dip sandwich). To drag your bread through a gravy or sauce is not only improper, but it also puts you at risk for a spill on your shirt!

Salads are easier to handle. If you are enjoying a salad as your main entrée for lunch, use your dinner fork. If you are having a salad before a main entrée, then use your salad fork, which is the smaller of the two. Some restaurants only set a table at lunchtime with one fork and one knife, and your waiter will bring you any additional silverware as needed, based on your order.

It is perfectly acceptable to cut your salad if the pieces are large. I will never forget a time when I was a teenager and a girlfriend and I were having lunch in a restaurant. She was eating a fruit salad. (This was in the days before we had fresh fruit available in every restaurant, particularly coffee shops.) Her salad consisted of lettuce, cottage cheese, canned peaches, and canned pears. My friend picked up a half of a canned pear (which one would normally cut into at least four pieces, maybe more) and proceeded to put the entire piece into her mouth. It looked a lot like when someone is trying to be funny by putting his or her fist in his or her mouth. Being a teenager and not realizing that I would embarrass her, I shrieked, "What are you *doing?*" When she finally had managed to get the pear down without choking, she said she didn't think it was polite to use a knife to cut her salad. What was so sweet was that she was practically gagging herself because she was trying to do what was proper etiquette, and instead made a faux pas. That is just one more reason why it is so important, especially in business, to have *some* basic knowledge of what is acceptable and what is not.

If you are ever served anything that is too big to put into your mouth, whether it is a pear in a salad, or a giant cheeseburger, it is acceptable to cut it into bite-sized pieces, one piece at a time. If you use your knife with your salad or appetizer, you can ask your waiter for a clean knife when he or she is clearing the table in preparation for serving your entrees.

Pay attention to your guests, too, and request clean silverware for them when necessary. If you are at a formal dinner, and you are being served your salad after the main course, your salad fork will be inside your dinner fork, directly next to the dinner plate. You may have had another small fork to the outside, which you would have used with your appetizer. Also, at a formal dinner, you may be served a sorbet between courses. This will be served with a small spoon. It is meant to cleanse your palate and prepare you for the next course. You do not have to eat all of it, but you should at least have a taste.

When you are served your entrée, eat it using your large fork and knife. Never cut more than one or two pieces at a time. As I mentioned earlier, when you have finished, place your utensils fully across the plate at an angle, as though connecting the 10 with the four on a clock. This should signal your waiter that you have finished eating.

For dessert, your waiter will usually bring you the necessary silverware when he serves you. It is customary to use a fork for cake or pie and a spoon for ice cream, mousse, crème brûlée, or other creamy dessert.

Try to never order anything that might be challenging to eat. Remember, though, that if you are ever served something that looks more challenging that you thought it would be, you can always ask your waiter for help. As the host, keep an eye on your guests, and always offer help if you think it is needed. I used to delight in telling clients that if they would like to order a whole lobster, the waiters can take it out of the shell for them. The look of relief on their faces told me how much they appreciated the suggestion.

Problem foods

Many foods come with their own set of problems. For example, if you eat an olive that still has the pit in it, remove the pit discreetly with your thumb and forefinger, and set it on the side of your plate. The same goes for shrimp tails. It is okay to pick up a large shrimp and eat it as finger food, taking one or two bites. Then place the tails on the side of your plate. If you are eating something with bones, whether it is poultry or fish, do the same. And if you ever encounter any other unwanted food item or by-product, simply remove it discreetly using your forefinger and thumb and put it on your plate. You should never spit food into your napkin. If possible, try to conceal it on your plate with a piece of food or garnish. If you haven't mastered chopsticks, request a fork with Asian cuisine.

Sometimes things are going to go wrong. In every case, you will want to handle them as discreetly as possible. Do you ever seem to be the one who finds foreign objects in your food? If that happens to you when you are with clients, tell your waiter discreetly and ask for something else. If it happens to your clients, act as the go-between for your table. Alert the waiter and ask that he or she bring your guest something else.

It is best not to take a chance with undercooked food, (especially poultry or pork). If your client orders steak or a burger, always ask him or her if it is cooked to his or her satisfaction. If it is undercooked or overcooked, it is your responsibility to flag down the waiter and resolve the situation. When you take clients out to lunch, you are the host or hostess. Your responsibilities are the same as if you invited your guests to your home for a meal.

At a recent business lunch, I ordered a luncheon filet to be cooked medium. It was a very thick steak and it came out rare, at best. I asked our waitress to please have it cooked a little more. My client commented afterward on how rude our waitress was, because as she returned my steak, she said, "That's a perfect medium, now." Well, it really wasn't. It was still as rare as ever. I ate the outside part that was cooked a little more, but left the majority of the steak, as it was too rare for my taste. I didn't want to make a fuss in front of my client.

The waitress assumed that she knew how I liked my steak and never came back to check up on me after she brought the steak back. She had been rude from the beginning, and she let us know that she was "very busy." She could have ruined our lunch, but I didn't let her. If I ever got her as my waitress at that restaurant again, I would discreetly approach the hostess and ask for someone else. Why take a chance on having bad service? This is one more reason to frequent restaurants that offer consistent quality and great service.

If you or a guest should happen to drop your silverware or your napkin at any time during your meal, don't pick it up! That is the waiter's responsibility. (The only exception to this is if there is the possibility that a utensil that was dropped could harm someone. I won't stand on ceremony if a knife falls in the middle of a busy pathway and someone could slip on it—or if someone could step on a fork. You get the idea.) You can wave to your waiter or a bus person, tell him what happened, and request a clean utensil. I will occasionally grab a clean utensil for my client from a nearby, unoccupied table if I don't see my waiter, and my client's food has already been served.

If ever you don't like what is served at a formal party, it is polite to at least take a taste. However, it is okay to not eat everything put before you if you don't care for it, or if you happen to be allergic to any particular food.

When you are done eating, and have placed your silverware across the middle of your plate, an experienced waiter will see that as a sign that you have finished. A lot of people (waiters and diners alike) don't know that a waiter should never begin to clear a table until everyone at the table has finished. As I discussed in a previous chapter, if your guests are done eating, and you are not, you should stop. But if you are the first to finish, sit patiently and contribute to the conversation so that your client can finish eating.

Never stack dishes at a table, and *never* push your plate away. The urge to do so is strong for some people (either they were encouraged as children to help clear the table, or they feel the need to push their plate away to stop themselves from eating more). Whatever the reason, and as well-intentioned as it may be, it is wrong to touch the plates in a restaurant. Be patient! And if your waiter attempts to remove anyone's plate or silverware before *everyone* has finished, it is your responsibility as the host to wave him or her away. Your guests will appreciate the gesture.

Although I suggested earlier that you might want to order coffee or tea, in order to have something to "play" with while your client finishes eating, you may prefer to wait until your guest is done. Avoid any action that may signal to your client that he or she needs to hurry through the rest of his or her meal.

Knowing the proper etiquette for business lunches will make you more comfortable with your clients and will make your clients more comfortable with you! When you exhibit proper etiquette, you will impress your clients by showing them that you know how to take good care of them. Your clients are likely to make the assumption that if you can take such good care of them at lunch, you will also take good care of them in business.

Chapter 14

Dining for Dollars: The Job Interview Luncheon

*Outshine your
competition by exhibiting
your best qualities.*

Y̶ou've submitted your resume. You've been called in for an interview. You think everything went perfectly. They said they'd be in touch. Then, instead of getting a phone call saying you got the job, you receive a call inviting you to lunch with the president, manager, owner, or some other individual who would likely be your boss should you make the grade.

If you are already starting to feel the onset of an anxiety attack just reading this, relax. You will be fine. In fact, you will be better than fine—you will be sensational! Once you understand *why* you have been invited to lunch, you will realize that you are most likely in the home stretch.

Let me start by saying this: It's *not* about lunch. And it's *not* about friendship. There may be many different reasons why a job interview will take place at a luncheon or dinner:

- To judge you on your social skills and manners.

- To find out additional information about you that an employer may not legally be able to ask.

- To get to know you better.

- To compare your social behavior to that of other candidates.

Think about it. What can employers accomplish at lunch that they can't in the office? That is what they are looking for: a degree of finesse that will separate you from the other candidates.

I have to reference the game of golf again, as it is the most revealing activity in which I have ever participated. I have met many people that I really liked—*until* I played golf with them. Their lack of sportsmanship, their temper, and their ethics are all revealed by this wonderful game. Conversely, I have known people that I didn't think I would like—*until* I played golf with them! Their good sportsmanship, conduct, and social skills made the game a joy, and left me with a new, favorable opinion of them as a people. Lunch can do the same thing for people.

A general manager at a local radio station once told me about a man he interviewed to be a sales manager in a neighboring market. He took the candidate to one of his favorite restaurants, where the candidate was brusque and abrasive to the server. The man's behavior cost him the job. This is *exactly* the kind of thing employers are looking for when they choose to interview a candidate at a restaurant.

Michele Tell, president of a public relations and marketing firm, originally had a difficult time finding employees who could handle the flexibility required by the fast pace of her tremendously successful company. You can try to explain a business to someone, but if he or she hasn't experienced it firsthand, he or she really doesn't know how crazy and chaotic it can be to work in publicity and public relations. There is the occasional outdoor event that gets cancelled due to weather, entertainment venues that get moved because the shows are not ready, restaurant openings that get delayed, and so on. In one case, Michelle had to have her staff call 400 people to reschedule an event. If you are not flexible, you will never make it in this field.

She solved her problem by scheduling lunch interviews with qualified candidates, as a follow-up to the office interview. She really separates the "men from the boys" when she cancels the lunch date just an hour before the scheduled rendezvous and then offers to reschedule. How the candidates handle that change is a good indication as to whether he or she will be able to deal effectively with the changes that present themselves in the PR industry.

If you are ever invited to interview during a business lunch, keep in mind that you are being judged on how you respond to everything that comes up—from how you handle bad service, to a change of venue, date, or time.

Always respond in the most polite, flexible, kind, caring way and you will outshine the other candidates. It's a good opportunity for you, too, to judge the behavior of your prospective employer. Do you want to work for someone who is rude to your server? Are the restaurant employees happy to wait on this "regular" customer? What if your interviewer knocks back a couple of beers at lunch, and expects you to do the same? A job interview business lunch is the *perfect* opportunity to learn things about people, or a relationship, that could affect your future and your livelihood.

Become a chameleon

Charles Clawson II, vice president of Commonwealth Title, told me about a time when he had taken a candidate to a local restaurant for an interview. He was looking for escrow officers for his company. Having to staff a new office from the ground up required that Charles interview people for every position. He confessed that he sometimes had *four* lunch appointments in *one* day!

He is a firm believer in the "job interview business lunch," because being out in a restaurant will reveal so much more of a candidate's personality than an office meeting. Anyone willing to go to such lengths as four lunches a day knows that sharing a meal with someone will reveal his or her personality faster and more effectively than all the office interviews in the world.

This particular candidate, a woman, made two mistakes that cost her a job with Charles. The two mistakes each indicated that she was "out of her league." The first thing she did wrong was to share that she was "so nervous!" It's one thing to be nervous if it is your first time on television, or your first time skydiving! It's even understandable to be nervous at a job interview. But it is inappropriate to mention it at that job interview—especially for a position that is going to involve constant client contact, and the ability to instill confidence in your clients. Charles said it has happened to him more than once—having people confess that they are nervous—and he detests hearing it.

We may all feel nervous or anxious when we are being judged, as in an interview, but we need to keep our emotions under control.

The second thing the candidate did wrong was to go on and on about the fabulous dessert tray. Charles said it wasn't just that she liked or enjoyed the desserts. It was the way she went on about them. They were not at a high-end restaurant, but an upscale—though casual—neighborhood restaurant. He said the desserts were good, but not the *best*. He had me in stitches as he imitated her—rolling his eyes and crooning, "Mmmmm, this dessert is *wonderful*.... It's so *creeeeeamy* and good!"

He said he was mortified at how this woman might act in front of his clients. So, though you always want to be appreciative of good food and good service, you need to act as though you have enjoyed this level of service a million times. You need to become a chameleon, able to rise above your level, or to go below, in an effort to fit in and make your future employer or clients comfortable.

Charles also shared with me that he had even been stood up once on a job interview luncheon! Do I even need to express here that if you *want* the job, you first have to *show up* for the interview? People talk, especially within a specific industry. Any candidate who would be a "no call, no show" on any job interview may have a hard time finding a job with *any* company in that industry, as the word about his or her "disappearing act" can get around.

A job interview luncheon is also a great opportunity for an employer to get a glimpse at your personal and professional life that he or she may not otherwise be able to witness. My former associate, Barry Berlin, told me about a job interview luncheon he had when he was employed as an account executive in New York.

Barry was interviewing with the advertising manager and general manager of East/West Network, the publisher of many "in-flight" magazines. They were at an exclusive New York City restaurant for lunch. During the luncheon, several well-known media people and publishing types walked in, and all of them came up to Barry to say "hello." The managers who were interviewing him were very impressed that he seemed to know "everyone" in the industry. Of course, he got the job!

Similarly, a friend of mine was interviewing for a job at a university. After the interview, she was invited out for Chinese food with three of the five panel members who had interviewed her. One of them was bilingual—speaking English and Spanish. During lunch, they informally spoke in Spanish. My friend said it was very natural, and she ended up feeling a good connection with them. She reflected that it would have been out of place for her to speak Spanish during the interview, but it was fun to do so during lunch. She believes it was probably a factor in her getting the job. Being bilingual was not a minimum qualification for the position, but it was definitely desirable.

This is a perfect example of why an interviewer might want to take a candidate out to lunch before making a decision. Lunch affords the opportunity to learn more about a candidate, whether or not what the interviewer learns is one of the requirements of the position.

Learn all you can about your interviewer

Here's an important tip when being interviewed, *especially* over lunch: Though your potential employer is looking to learn more about *you,* you can better prepare yourself for the luncheon by learning more about *him or her*! With the convenience of the Internet, this has become a very simple task. But be careful—there are no guarantees that you will find exactly who you are looking for, as the following example proves.

Teri Marshall left Las Vegas after two hard years of trying to find success in sales. In her own words, "I went running back to my home town in the San Francisco Bay Area faster than you can say 'Tony Bennett,' and went to work trying to regain my foothold in the print advertising sales profession."

Teri soon found out that one of the top publishing companies in the country needed a new rep for its portfolio of national consumer magazines, a position for which she would be perfectly suited (her background included work as a sales rep for a major trade magazine publisher). As happens so many times during an interview process, we are made to feel we have the job, only to find out that there are still more hurdles over which to jump. She had a verbal offer and then found out she had to survive a phone interview with the corporate director in New York. She did what most savvy salespeople would do, and "Googled" her prospective executive to learn everything about him that she could before the big telephone interview.

Her "Mr. New York" came up as an avid hunter, who also coached a women's lacrosse team at a Catholic college on the east coast. She became concerned as she failed to find any common interests between herself and this man, but she also wasn't finding much about him that she even liked—Teri was upset because hunters kill animals, and lacrosse is an extremely forceful sport!

Still, after a very challenging phone interview, Teri was hired, and she flew out to meet "Mr. New York" immediately. She had eight meetings that day, including breakfast and lunch meetings, after arriving on a red-eye flight. She recalled that breakfast went smoothly, and she had listened a lot (one of the hardest things for a salesperson to do). After a few more meetings she went on to lunch.

A few of the executives ordered wine, but she followed the lead of "Mr. New York" and ordered bottled water. Many times throughout the day she fought the urge to mention the hunting or lacrosse. She thought it could be a fun ice-breaker, but it could also backfire if her new boss wanted to keep his private life private. At that point, she felt it was hard to tell how well this group knew each other, so she decided it was inappropriate to ask the question at lunch.

By the end of the day, after a solid 11 hours of nonstop meetings, enough comments had passed so that it was abundantly clear that she shared a similar sense of humor with "Mr. New York." She finally asked the question. Was he the same man who enjoyed killing Bambi and coaching lacrosse? He practically fell to the floor from laughing so hard! Because she had waited so long to ask him about his personal life, he was comfortable enough with her to let loose. He thought she was great and he couldn't wait to share her "Google" story with everyone he knew.

Incidentally, he later asked Teri if she had ever "Googled" herself, which she had not. It turned out there is someone who shared her maiden name, who has his own Website. He's a transvestite in London. So, while going on a mission to research the company or executives for whom you might like to work, keep in mind that the World Wide Web is huge. You may find others of the same name. Regardless of the mix-up, her new boss was ultimately impressed that she had taken the time to research him, and had found a great anecdote in the process.

Another lesson that Teri's experience reinforces is that timing is everything. The fun of this occasion might have been lost if she had blurted out the question at lunch. She did the right thing in waiting for a more appropriate time.

Speaking of timing, you remember the story about my friend Janice, who lost more than $60,000 in commissions because she was late to a presentation? Well, one of the few things that is worse than being late for a meeting is being late for a job interview!

Dr. Dennis Myers, "The Management Chef," was looking for a job more than 30 years ago, but said he remembers what happened to him as if it had been yesterday. With no employment prospects and a pregnant wife, he was more than thrilled when his phone rang and a former employer wanted to meet him for lunch that day. Dennis jumped at the chance—even though he knew he would have to hurry to get ready for the meeting and make it up to Los Angeles (60 miles away from his home).

He agreed on a time to meet at his boss's favorite restaurant, and he confirmed that he knew the location. Once there, he nursed his water past the point of embarrassment, and finally asked the waiter for help. The waiter told him there were *two* restaurants with the *same* name on this street! What are the odds of that happening?

His assumption put him in the wrong restaurant. By the time he finally blew into the right restaurant, his interviewer was on his third martini. As the luncheon deteriorated, both still realized there was a match of talent and need. The employer said he would call soon.

It wasn't long before Dennis got the call to meet this man for dinner. Dennis sat with his wife by his side while he answered the exact same questions the man had asked him earlier (while inebriated). When his boss finally asked Dennis if *he* had any questions, Dennis responded, "I have one—when are you going to get around to hiring me?" The employer laughed, and then offered him a job with reinstatement of his service record and benefits.

Dennis's story contains three significant messages. First, it is a great reminder to always confirm the location of your meeting, whether it is a fabulous new restaurant, or your old standard. Never leave anything to chance!

Secondly, in the old three-martini days, very little was accomplished that didn't have to be done over.

And finally, if you want something, ask for it! I have heard from many people that the one question they asked at an interview that got them the job was, "When are you going to hire me?" You might be more comfortable asking your interviewer, "Where do we go from here?" or "What's our next step?" But ask.

You might also want to offer to pick up the check. Any company that is interviewing during lunch can write off the expense (and should, by all means, pay for the lunch). But it is polite for you to offer. Whether you get to pay or not, always follow up with a thank-you note.

Chapter 15

Networking Luncheons: The Successful Professional's Gold Mine

Fight the urge to
retreat to your
comfort zone.

The usual scenario

I'm sure if you've ever been to a networking event you have probably entered the room or restaurant where it was being held and immediately gravitated to your friends, colleagues, or associates. You may have even called someone beforehand, to see if he or she was going, so that you could plan on sitting together, or seeing him or her there.

Then, you may have sat down with your friends and associates. Usually there is a business card exchange at the start of such an event, where each person at your table is expected to pass his or her card out to everyone else at the table. You probably already know most of the guests at your table. You *may* make the acquaintance of someone who happens to be sitting at your table—someone who works somewhere interesting or for a company where a friend of yours works. You may find an easy opening to begin a conversation, or you may not.

You and your friend (the one you called earlier so that you wouldn't have to get through this alone) now get to enjoy the breakfast or lunch, and listen to a guest speaker. When the speaker has finished their presentation, you leave to go back to work.

Did you meet anyone new? Maybe a friend of yours introduced you to a colleague, or someone from his or her office. Maybe you left with little more than a full stomach, business cards from the other guests at your table, and a little bit of knowledge or inspiration that you gained from listening to the speaker.

Sound familiar? Do you think this is taking advantage of a networking luncheon to the best of your ability? Is it moving your business along at a faster pace? Or are you simply resigned to paying $30 for some bacon and eggs, or a chicken salad with a side of inspiration?

I don't blame you one bit. No matter *how* gregarious you might be, or how outgoing you *usually* are with your friends, networking functions take a lot of courage and energy. I can remember coming home from many such functions feeling absolutely wiped out. It's hard to be "on," meet and greet everyone, and try to remember names.

I used to feel that if I came away with one or two new acquaintances I had done well. That was a long, long time ago. Once I learned how to really take advantage of net-working luncheons, I actually started to look forward to them! You too can make the change, and discover how to get the most out of these events.

Even *you* can learn to *love* networking!

Some of the best advice to overcome any insecurity or discomfort you may feel is to act as though you are the host or hostess. If it was *your* party, what would you do differently? I have been networking in Las Vegas for more than 20 years now, and most of the time I can joke that it's like being at my own wedding, or any other party where I would know at least half of the guests! That's what we are actually trying to accomplish—to become so well-con-nected that even if we don't know everyone, we at least "know someone, who knows someone, who...." Acting as a host or hostess helps to alleviate a lot of the stress of being new to a group, or new in a particular field.

I get to experience the phenomenon of successful networking every day of my life. I have helped people find jobs, recommended the best places to go for a business lunch, suggested where to find the best hair stylist, massage therapist, chiropractor, dentist, and so on. If I don't know someone who can help, I'm willing to bet I know someone *else* who knows someone who can help. And through this reciprocal process we all become "in the know"!

However, I understand how challenging this type of networking can be if you are more introverted. So, the next time you are attending a networking function, whether it is a breakfast, a lunch, a dinner, or a mixer, take my advice and pretend that it is your party. Ask a stranger if you can freshen up his or her drink. Bring a carafe of orange juice or coffee over to your table at a breakfast meeting, and go around the table offering to pour everyone a glass.

I've often started a conversation by telling people they look familiar—followed by "What do you do?" or "Where do you work?" They will always tell me. What do you have to be afraid of? Everyone else is likely to be feeling just as uncomfortable. Most people are thrilled to have someone come up to them and engage them in a conversation. Then, if you meet someone in a related field, invite him or her out to lunch. It's as simple as that! There's no easier way to meet new people, especially when you want to expand your business prospects.

This technique applies to both those who own a business, and those who work for others. I know so many people who improved their networking habits once they took ownership of a business. Suddenly, it seemed a whole lot more important to succeed. Shyness became a luxury they could no longer afford. When you *need* to grow your business and become more successful, you will find it much easier to dive right in. Whenever you work for yourself (as opposed to working for a company that you don't own), you will find yourself increasingly motivated to mingle. However, if you happen to be working for someone else, keep in mind that *his* or *her* success will become *your* success, and vice versa. Pretend you own the company you work for, and one day you might!

If you go to networking events with the intention of meeting as many people as possible, you will begin to find the events more rewarding, both personally and professionally. Plus think about all the people who need to meet *you!* If you are successful in your field, then people will be as excited to meet you as you are to meet them.

We all have to fight the urge to cling to that which is familiar. Perhaps you don't get to see enough of your friends or associates, and so you feel that a networking luncheon is the perfect opportunity to catch up. If that's the case, try to get there early, or even stay late, in order to visit with your friends. (And remember that seeing your friends should not be your main motivation for attending any networking event.) You might even consider inviting your friends to go out for coffee after a networking luncheon, thereby freeing yourself up to make new acquaintances *during* the event. I've even taken friends to dinner after a mixer. Once you learn how to really take advantage of networking events, and how to use them to build your business, you will begin to see them in a different light.

I attended a luncheon that featured Jill Lublin, co-author of *Networking Magic* (Adams Media Corporation, 2004) and *Guerrilla Publicity* (Adams Media Corporation, 2002), as the guest speaker. During the event, she had each of us think of an area in which we needed help—whether it was finding a landscaper, hiring a new secretary, or locating donors for an upcoming silent auction. Then, Lublin instructed us to ask every other person at our table (tables of six), "Who do you know who _____?"

Even after networking for more than 20 years, this was still an incredible experience for me. Doing this exercise forced everyone at each table to share what they were working on, or what they were looking for, with the other people at our table. It took traditional networking—a brief introduction and exchange of business cards—to a much higher level, one that included learning about the others that were seated at our table.

Next she asked each of us to reveal something about ourselves that few people knew. Think about that. What would you say? Personally, I feel as though my life is an open book (having lived and worked in my community for so long). Everywhere I go I run into people I know. So, it was a very challenging exercise for me. I came up with something minor at the time, but as soon as the exercise was finished, my mind flooded with personal things that few people in my industry know about me. I realized afterward that it would have been fun to share that I am certified to do energy healing. That is exactly the kind of conversation starter that you should be prepared to talk about—an interesting subject that will stimulate discussions.

Did you just return from a trip to Russia? Did your daughter win a beauty pageant? Did you just take a cooking class on Indian cuisine? You never know what subject someone else might find fascinating. Now, what if you were to do that with *everyone* who is in a room with you? You can! Be prepared to discuss exciting and different things. As I mentioned earlier, watching a national news program in the morning, reading topical journals and magazines, and doing your research so that you can be ready for any casual or business conversation will always give you an edge, *especially* at a networking event.

Jill recommends that you be *intentional* about what you would like to create or gain from any networking event.

"Before I enter any room, I create my goals and intentions," she later told me. "For trade shows and conferences I write them down, keep them with me, and look at them every day. These actions will guarantee better networking results."

You get back what you give—and then some!

A great way to expand your networking connections is to find out what professional organizations cater to your industry, and participate in them religiously. You might, perhaps, volunteer on a committee. I am a former president of Las Vegas Women in Communications (WIC), and I have served on the board of directors for WIC, off and on, for the past 17 years. When I am at a WIC luncheon, it is as if I'm at my own home. I always know more than half of the guests, and I always have a wonderful experience. I highly recommend becoming *involved* in your networking organizations, instead of just attending the meetings.

Of course you may not have time to serve on more than one board or committee, but participating will help you to overcome any networking jitters you may have, and I guarantee that you will make new friends along the way. If you don't have time to serve on a board, then you might consider volunteering to work on a committee. Or maybe volunteer to help at the check-in desk at a mixer (that's one way to meet everyone there!). Serve on a calling committee, pass out brochures, or find some way to work for your organizations whenever you can. The benefits outweigh the time and effort.

When I was the director of education for WIC, I not only had to book the speakers, but I had to stand up and introduce them at the luncheons. I held that position for three years. Believe me when I say that I found doing this in my second- and third-year terms much easier to do than in the first. I can remember being so nervous the first year that my lips would stick to my teeth! Now when I address large groups, I rarely even get nervous. When you volunteer, you *will* get back what you put in...and then some! And remember: If you go beyond working on a committee, and actually join a board of directors, you will put yourself in the position to direct the course of the organization.

Before you attend any function, develop a strong, interesting sound bite. As I mentioned in Chapter 3, a sound bite is a brief introduction of who you are, and what you do. It paves the way for discovering common ground or mutual acquaintances. If you are an interior designer and you just did a makeover for someone, I'm sure that would be of interest to a lot of people—especially in light of the popularity of home-makeover television shows! Whatever you do in your career, there is something about it that will be of interest to others. Share a little bit about yourself, and you will learn a lot about other people.

And keep in mind that you want to attend functions with the *intention* of meeting some new people. Honoree Corpron, an author and business coach, says that whenever she enters a room at a networking event, she can immediately spot at least five people she wants to meet. This is not based on who looks well-heeled, but more on who looks as if they *care* about being there. Even if you are on a tight budget, you can still clean up and dress neatly, and appear eager to make a good impression with the new people you are going to meet.

Look at the guests in the room and pick out some of the people who look most interesting to you, and who look as though they are interested in being there. Introduce yourself to them with a great, sincere sound bite that shares who you are, where you work, and what you do. Then ask them what they do. You want to make sure that your introduction is sincere and paves the way for good communication. Always focus on the person to whom you are talking.

Never be what Keith Ferrazzi terms a "Networking Jerk." In his book, *Never Eat Alone* (Currency, 2005), he describes the Networking Jerk as a person with business cards in one hand, a drink in the other, with "an elevator pitch always at the ready." He or she "is a schmooze artist, eyes darting at every event in a constant search for a bigger fish to fry."

When you meet someone of interest, make a note on the back of his or her business card that includes the event where you met, along with any other pertinent information. Send him or her an e-mail, and put him or her in your database with any personal notes. As you build your networking database, remember to use it when necessary. I love it when someone calls me for a referral.

With a little practice, you will begin to look forward to your networking luncheons and events. Developing a great introduction, volunteering to serve on a board or a committee, and assuming the role of host or hostess will help you to overcome any reluctance you have about networking. Take advantage of the opportunity that effective networking offers, and watch your business grow!

Chapter 16

Farewells and Follow-Ups

Thank your clients for
taking the time to have
lunch with you.

Lunch is finished. Now what? You'll likely either end up by saying good-bye outside the restaurant, or by returning your client to his or her office. I always make sure to tell my clients how much I enjoyed going to lunch with them, regardless of whether it was our first time meeting, or one of many lunches we've had together. Then I thank *them* for taking the time to have lunch with me. You may think this is absurd, because I was the one who took them to lunch. You might think your clients should thank you for taking them to lunch, especially if you didn't talk specifically about business, or try to "sell" them anything.

Distinguish yourself from the crowd

It is very important to remember that relationships are built on how people feel about you, as well as how they feel about being with you. If you are always gracious and thank your clients for taking time out of their busy day to spend it with you, they will like how you have made them feel about themselves, and they will want to spend more time with you. Then, hopefully, the next time you invite them to lunch, they will jump at the chance because what they will remember most will likely be how they felt the last time they were with you. All of these feelings build the foundation for long-lasting relationships.

Francine Prose published an interesting article in *O Magazine* about learning to trust your gut reaction. She said that her friend, California filmmaker Freude Bartlett, had given her advice about how to choose her friends, and I believe this can be dead-on with regard to choosing business relationships as well. Bartlett's advice was that whenever you've just spent time with a particular person, ask yourself, "Do I feel better or worse than I did before?" She continued the advice by emphasizing that you should not consider any explanations or excuses, just "better" or "worse."

This is a marvelous method for choosing your friends, and if you try it in your personal life, I'm sure you will begin to make some changes. But, if you put yourself in your client's position and you apply it to business, think about the impact you can have in your clients' lives. If they come away from spending time with you and they feel "better," they will want to spend more time with you—whether they consciously realize it or not.

Think about the relationships in your life. Do you want to pursue relationships with people who are critical of you, or who make you question yourself? Do you want to grow closer to someone who is not a pleasure to be around? Think about the friends in your life and your closest business associates. Do you laugh with them? Do you have fun with them? Do you prefer to do business with some of them more than with others? Why is that? Give some deep thought to the relationships that you enjoy the most. What are the qualities of those associations? How did they begin?

If you've ever had a bad or uncomfortable lunch with a client, how long is it before you invite him or her to lunch again? Or, have you ever been on the other side of the fence, when someone invited you to lunch and you didn't have a pleasant experience? Would you bother to go with him or her again if you didn't have to? Try to be the kind of person that your clients will be anxious to spend time with.

I can remember when I had just started working at the highway radio station, and I went to lunch with someone who had been a client of mine when I was my employed by a television station. I had hoped to keep him as an advertiser now that I was in radio.

He had asked me to take him to lunch at a Mexican restaurant. When I did, he proceeded to complain about everything, and not just the lunch. He had broken his foot. His daughter was being difficult. His business was in a slump. He complained about politics, business, his competition, and his clients. He never stopped griping all throughout our lunch. We finally left the restaurant and said good-bye, after what seemed to me to be the longest lunch in history.

My very next stop was at a drug store to buy something for an upset stomach. Between the spicy food and his complaining, I had let him make me sick. It was a while before I invited him to lunch again. Can you imagine someone thinking about *you* in the same way that I thought about him? Why would anybody want to be around such a negative person?

We all need to vent sometimes, and it is important to listen and to offer a sympathetic ear, which I did for this client. Life is not always a bed of roses. Being there to help and support your clients when they are going through a hard time can offer you a tremendous opportunity to bond with them. Remember that you don't want to be there just when things are going smoothly. I always pride myself on the fact that I can listen, and be supportive and helpful.

So, whereas you don't have to be a stand-up comedian or an entertainer to be good at taking people to lunch, you do have to be considerate and sincere. Be great company and they will want to spend time with you. You have to cater to your client's wishes, and be there for them in every way. You need to listen to them when they need to talk.

Always follow up a client lunch with a thank-you note. I am frequently asked if sending an e-mail will suffice. Personally, I love to get thank-you notes in the mail. Don't you? A former boss, Bill Utton, taught me that people *love* to get something in the mail that isn't a bill! It's true, too. And an e-mail just doesn't carry the weight of a handwritten note.

Send it out as soon as you get back to your desk. It can be a simple "thank you" that shows you are sincere. For example: "Hi, Bob. I just wanted to thank you for your time today. I am looking forward to working with you. Please feel free to call me if you have any questions. See you soon, Robin." Or you can add something more personal, or something targeted to what you talked about at lunch: "Have a great golf game this weekend. Let me know how the course plays." Or, "I hope your son's birthday party is perfect!" Keep it light and simple, but try to add something that pertains to your lunch conversation, as it will let him or her know that you were listening, and that you care.

If any business questions came up during your lunch, follow up as soon as possible with a phone call, fax, or e-mail. It's another way to show how much you care about your business, your clients, and your relationships with them. Developing a good follow-up routine is a great way to pull ahead of your competition.

The Final Word

Breaking bread will

help you to earn

more dough!

We all have a tendency to want to stay in our comfort zones. Once you learn to break away from your business comfort zone, you will open up a whole new world of relationships and success.

It's always great to see your friends or associates socially, but you really can't afford to miss the opportunity to share a meal with a client or a business associate. Once you break bread with someone, you transform that relationship and personalize it. Nothing else can compare to the magic that happens when you share a meal with another human being.

Business lunches can become an incredibly rewarding and entertaining way of doing business. Nearly everything covered in my book also applies to breakfast meetings, dinners, cocktail parties, and mixers. We each have more than 500 opportunities each year to build better relationships! What could *you* do with 500 chances to improve your business by building better relationships?

Hopefully, with practice, you will begin to enjoy taking clients to lunch as much as I always have. When given the choice to meet a client at a restaurant or at his or her office, I will always choose a restaurant! The atmosphere is so much more favorable for building relationships. You will learn more about your clients, their businesses, their goals—and you will even learn more about yourself!

Always remember, though, to never let your guard down. Even though the atmosphere is more relaxed, it is still a business meeting. With time and experience, you will learn to overcome any insecurities or uncertainties you may have about what you can, or cannot, accomplish during lunch. It really does come down to the fact that the more you get used to meeting at a table, the more relaxed you will become at business lunches. Hopefully, most of your lunches with clients will work to turn your business relationships into long-lasting, solid friendships.

Another reason that I prefer to meet over a meal, rather than in a conference room or office, is because of the factor of fun in the air. For someone who is in his or her office all day, getting out for a business lunch can provide a much-needed break. When you consistently take good care of your clients, and their businesses, they will come to associate you not only with a good time, but they will think of you as someone who helps move their business forward. I hope that you will practice what you have learned and gain an increased awareness of the "dance" that occurs when you share a business lunch.

Watch, listen, and learn. Ask questions, and really get to know the people you are working with. I once had a client share something with me that she had learned at a seminar she had attended more than 10 years ago. She said, "If you ever don't like someone, get to know them." That is good advice, whether for business or your personal life. I'm so glad that my client, Cindy, shared that pearl of wisdom with me, because it has enabled me to find the likeable side of people in my industry—even those clients who are not generally popular. I can now see the fear that drives them, the upbringing that molded them, and the reasons behind the things that make them tick.

Many times I've mentioned to colleagues that I had a great lunch with someone who may have an unfriendly reputation, and they have responded with scrunched-up faces, saying, "How can you stand him?"

I am always honest with my response when I explain that this person has a very interesting background. And I might share something I have learned about the person (though nothing of a confidential nature) that leaves my colleagues with a greater understanding about the person that they "don't like." So by getting to know someone, and what makes him or her tick, I not only improve my relationship with the person, but help to create a more understanding view of him or her within the industry.

In one such case, I worked with a client who was very particular about every detail, and who expected huge, complex proposals, at greatly discounted prices. Naturally, this frustrated many of her vendors, who were used to selling their products without much effort. However, I found out (by getting to know her over lunch) that she had come from a big family, and she had grown up fairly poor. She loved to plan, and she valued economy. Growing up as one of 10 children was often chaotic, and she didn't want her own adult life (or anything in it) to happen haphazardly. This client had actually found the ideal job for her personality (as a media planner). One day I asked her how long she had been at her current job and she replied, "Five quarters." Now that's a media planner!

I liked her after our first lunch, and we ended up having many more great lunches together. Once I learned what made her tick, and why she was the way she was, her attention to detail didn't bother me at all. In fact, I learned to appreciate it. Many people in our industry who were frustrated by her demands didn't understand how I got along so well with her. All I did was ask questions, listened to her answers, and get to know her!

And I'll admit, there are some clients who I don't enjoy taking to lunch, even after I have given it my best shot to get to know them. But because I believe so strongly in what can be accomplished by breaking bread with someone, I keep trying, hoping that some day he or she will relax, and "lighten up!" In the meantime, I continue to stop by with pastries, doughnuts, ice cream—anything we can share—in an attempt to take that relationship to a higher level.

Enjoy trying new things and new places. And when you take out a new client, be on your toes—but don't be nervous. Remember: Your clients or guests are as likely to be as uncomfortable as you might be. Especially in the beginning of your relationship! Learn how to make lunch fun. Practice on your friends.

Once you feel confident enough to invite a client to lunch, keep the following things in mind:

1. Establish a list of your favorite restaurants for business—restaurants that meet my "Top 10 Criteria" for choosing a perfect restaurant for a business lunch. This list is available on my Website (*www.RobinJay.com*), but doing the

research to create your own Top 10 list is a wonderful experience in itself! Remember to take your friends, not your clients, when trying someplace new.

2. Once you have your own list of great business-lunch restaurants, organize it by location. Have several suggestions ready when arranging to meet with clients, and always have your list in front of you when you are calling to confirm.

3. Make sure you have brushed up on your etiquette. You will want to feel confident about handling each aspect of your business lunch, from ordering for the table, to settling the check. If you are unsure about any aspect of etiquette, then review it before you make a lunch date with a client. There are many great books that cover the subject in some depth.

4. Prepare yourself for casual conversation by getting up to date on current events: news, the stock market, business, music, fashion, celebrities, entertainment, and so on. You want to be able to contribute something of interest, no matter where the conversation goes.

5. Have your business goals in order. What do you hope to accomplish at each luncheon? If you are making a formal presentation, have all of your materials ready. If your goal is to work on building a relationship, then be prepared to ask questions that will help you to discover common ground.

6. Determine your mode of transportation. If you are going to offer to pick up your client at his or her office, make sure your car is clean. If you are renting an exotic car or a limousine, confirm your arrangements.

7. Now go for it! Invite a client out to lunch.

8. Call your chosen restaurant to make a reservation the day before your scheduled luncheon.

9. The day of the luncheon, take it easy on fragrance, and remember to dress appropriately.

10. Pay attention to the clock. Communicate with your client before lunch so that you will be aware of his or her schedule, and pace the luncheon accordingly.

When you are done, keep track of your progress on paper. Did you have a nice lunch? Do you think your client enjoyed it? Did your client *tell* you he or she enjoyed it? Did *you* have fun? Did you accomplish your goals? Do you think your business lunch went better than a meeting at his or her office might have? If you attended a networking luncheon, what did you accomplish? Did you meet some interesting new people? Did you book any lunch dates with new associates? Did you follow up with an e-mail or a phone call? Was it easier than you thought it would be?

You will gain confidence each time that you achieve a positive outcome, and you will soon learn what pleases people the most, especially when it comes to a business lunch. Keeping a record of your business lunches—what happened, how they progressed, and what you would change next time—will help you to achieve greater results at future luncheons. Learn from your mistakes and repeat your successes.

We are all in this together. Sharing with other business professionals is the best way to build relationships. Discover for yourself how breaking bread with your clients will not only elevate your business relationships to a higher level, but will also fill your life with more joy.

Good luck
and
bon appetit!

Index

About the Author

ROBIN JAY worked as an advertising account manager for more than 18 years. She experienced a more-than 2,000-percent increase in sales in her career, largely because of her ability to build strong and lasting relationships. During her lengthy career she was awarded the Electronic Media Award for Radio Account Executive of the Year.

An expert on building business relationships, Jay found that bringing a social situation (particularly lunch) into business relationships works to bond client and salesperson. She attributes her proven track record to applying the lessons she learned during her vast experience courting clients. She has personally hosted more than 3,000 client lunches in her career, which has earned her the title of "The Queen of the Business Lunch."

A former president of Las Vegas Women in Communications (WIC), Jay has also served on its board of directors, as well as on the boards of The Advertising Community Talent Show (ACTS) and the Juvenile Diabetes Foundation.

Jay has written articles for Bacon's Information/Expert PR Newswire, *What's On*, *America West Magazine*, and *The Las Vegas Review-Journal*. She has also written advertising copy for such clients as the MGM Grand Hotel and the Sahara Hotel & Casino.

Jay currently works as a consultant, public speaker, and corporate trainer. In addition, she a faculty member of the University of Nevada, Las Vegas, the Educational Outreach program, and is also a Certified Reconnection Healing Practitioner.

Originally from Cleveland, Ohio, Jay has lived in Las Vegas, Nevada, for more than 30 years. She enjoys playing golf, singing, gardening, gourmet cooking, and sharing time with her dog Georgie.

For corporate training, coaching, and consulting, contact Robin Jay at *www.RobinJay.com*.